KU-626-523

LEON

HAPPY CURRIES

BY REBECCA SEAL & JOHN VINCENT

 conran
OCTOPUS

CONTENTS

INTRODUCTION.........................4

MILD 12

FIERY 36

CREAMY 58

SPEEDY.................................. 86

SLOW..................................... 126

SIDES..................................... 152

BREAD 196

PICKLES & CHUTNEYS 212

INDEX...................................218

ABOUT THE AUTHORS 222

ACKNOWLEDGEMENTS 223

KEY

WF
WHEAT FREE

GF
GLUTEN FREE

DF
DAIRY FREE

V
VEGETARIAN

Ve
VEGAN

NF
NUT FREE

SoF
SOY FREE

SUITABLE FOR FREEZING

INTRODUCTION

Did you know that in India there is no such thing as curry? Curry, seemingly that most Asian of all foods, was a word invented by Portuguese and British colonialists surrounded by exotic Indian foods in the fifteenth and sixteenth centuries. They used it to describe the unfamiliar food they encountered on their travels.

As a word its roots are uncertain, but at LEON we are fairly sure that it came from the Tamil 'kari', meaning 'grilled' or 'to bite and chew' or even just a kind of sauce (or possibly from a very old English word for stew). These various definitions have as much specificity as the modern 'curry', which, in English, describes everything from a rich, fragrant coconut-based soup to a bowl of spice-rubbed grilled meat – and everything in between. But in India, and across much of Asia, dishes we think of as curry are called by their own particular names.

Soon the idea of curry spread across the British and Portuguese Empires via sailors, traders and the Indian cooks who travelled with them. Bold flavours and spices were diluted to suit meeker British palates until *Mrs Beeton's Book of Household Management* recorded a recipe in 1861 that listed apples, cream and meat as the main ingredients (with just a dash of curry powder).

During the following centuries, as trade routes and whole communities of people crossed back and forth, the idea of curry spread even further – to the Caribbean, to southern Africa, to the islands of the Indian Ocean and the South Pacific, and adopted the sumptuous dishes of these countries too.

In this way, curry has become a magical world of exotic flavours and spice – and, at LEON, those are some of our favourite things. Curry can be so deliciously varied – fresh, light, healthy, sour, hot, creamy, mild, soothing or rich, and we wanted to create a collection of the very best we've tasted. We've found joy in our journey through spice and time, collecting recipes from friends, the LEON team, family, local restaurants and our travel diaries.

So really, curry can mean anything you want it to. We think that curry is many delicious, happy things. We hope you think so too.

Rebecca and John

STORECUPBOARD

SPICES

asafoetida

black mustard seeds

black peppercorns

black salt

green cardamom pods

cayenne pepper

chaat masala

dried chillies

dried red chilli flakes

hot chilli powder

cinnamon (whole sticks & ground)

cloves (whole)

coriander (seeds & ground)

cumin (seeds & ground)

curry powder (Caribbean & Madras)

fennel seeds

fenugreek seeds

dried fenugreek leaves (methi)

garam masala

ground mace

ground turmeric

mustard seeds

nigella seeds

whole nutmeg

paprika (sweet & smoked)

saffron

FREEZER

sustainable seafood

MSC-certified salmon fillets

lime leaves

fresh curry leaves

peas

fenugreek leaves (methi)

whole leaf spinach

ready-made paratha

ready-made naan

ready-made rotis/ chapatis

FRIDGE

high-welfare meat (ideally organic)

sustainably sourced fish

fish sauce

galangal paste

tamarind paste

ghee (can be vegan)

full-fat plain yoghurt (can be non-dairy)

paneer

good-quality Thai curry pastes

nam prik pao (Thai chilli paste)

extra-firm tofu (non-GMO/organic)

FRESH

lemons and limes

cauliflower

onions

spring onions

shallots

ginger

garlic

lemongrass

hot & mild chillies

Thai basil

coriander

mint

bay leaves

thyme

kale

sweet potatoes

green beans

organic/free-range eggs

CUPBOARD

canned tomatoes

passata

canned chickpeas

canned kala chana (black chickpeas)

canned kidney beans

canned black beans

full-fat coconut milk

desiccated coconut

sticky rice

basmati rice

mixed wild & basmati rice

black rice

jasmine rice

split peas

red lentils

split white urid dal/lentils

black urid dal/lentils

split yellow mung/moong dal/lentils

extra-firm tofu

noodles

chapati flour (atta)

unroasted cashew nuts

unroasted peanuts

neutral cooking oil (ideally rapeseed)

chickpea/gram flour (besan)

apple cider vinegar

canned unripe green jackfruit

CHOP CHOP

TIPS FOR SPEEDY CURRIES

- Get everything ready before you start – no rummaging around for cumin seeds while garlic burns in the pan.

- Keep your knives sharp for quicker prep.

- Set a bowl next to your chopping board, for the trimmings and scraps.

- Soak rice before it goes in the pan, to speed up its cooking time.

- Bags of frozen ready-made finely chopped onion from the supermarket are your friend.

- Instead of fresh, both ready-made frozen chopped garlic and ginger are great. You can also use ginger paste or garlic paste from a jar if you want, but we reckon they're best used in curries that get a good long cook, as they don't taste quite right in the quick-cook dishes.

- It's expensive, but (in a pinch) microwaveable rice is a major time-saver.

LEAVE IT TO THE PROS...

When we sat down to plan this book, we talked about including recipes for authentic homemade poppadums, prawn crackers and all sorts of other delicious things that we love to eat with curries. We do believe in the power of freshly home-made goodies...most of the time. But we also have busy families and full-time jobs (rather more than full-time, in John's case, running LEON!), so we are always on the lookout for hacks and short-cuts – as long as they still taste great.

We have included a recipe for samosas, as well as some for breads, pickles and chutneys, so do try them out, when you have the time (and we're in awe of you if you do). However, if you're passing a specialist shop, or even a big supermarket, you can easily stock up on fresh and frozen flatbreads, such as parathas and naan, and pastries, such as samosas (look out for frozen vegetable gyoza dumplings and vegetable spring rolls, too).

Frying your own poppadums or prawn crackers is easy and they are even more delicious than they are ready-made. Buy boxes of uncooked poppadum discs, or translucent uncooked prawn crackers, and cook for just a few seconds each in hot oil.

BASIC STEAMED WHITE RICE

SERVES 4

PREP TIME: UP TO 20 MINS SOAKING • COOK TIME: 12 MINS + STANDING TIME

WF • GF • DF • V • VE • NF • SF

240g **long-grain rice** (basmati or jasmine)

water

salt

== TIP ==

As a general rule, allow 60g uncooked rice per person and adjust recipe quantities accordingly.

You'll turn to this recipe time and time again as the perfect accompaniment for countless curries. People often think rice is difficult to get right but this method will make it perfect every time.

It really is worth washing the rice – it removes some of the starch on the outside of each grain, meaning you get nice, fluffy rice, rather than mushy, sticky rice. Don't cook it in masses of water either – less is more here.

We usually add water by eye, but if you prefer to measure the best ratio we have found is 2:1 by volume of water to rice – measure the rice onto your scales using a mug, keeping count of the number you fill, and then use the mug to measure double the amount of water for cooking.

Rinse the rice in several changes of cold water. If you're cooking basmati rice, then it will shorten the cooking time and improve the texture if you can soak the rice in cold water for 10–30 minutes, but it's not essential if you're pushed for time (or extremely hungry).

Drain the rice and place in a large pan with a tight-fitting lid. If you already measured the water add it now, or alternatively add cold water to the pan until it's about 2cm above the rice.

Add a pinch of salt then set the pan over a medium heat. Bring up to the boil, then cover with a lid and turn the heat down to a simmer. Cook for 12 minutes, then remove from the heat and remove the lid. Check the texture – it should be almost completely cooked, but if it's unsoaked basmati, then it might need a dash more water and 2 more minutes. If it's ready, fluff up the rice with a fork then cover again and leave to steam until you are ready to serve.

SPICE IT UP

SPICE BLENDS

We recommend roasting and grinding or blending spices wherever possible, but sometimes there just isn't time. And some recipes, like Japanese curry, are almost always made with a ready-made blend. We keep a stash of mild Madras curry powder and a subtly – but importantly – different tub of Caribbean curry powder, as well as garam masala. For each, it's worth seeking out a really good brand from a specialist shop or online.

HOW TO LOOK AFTER SPICES

Although no spice lasts indefinitely, keeping them in a cool, dark cupboard, and in airtight containers, will lengthen their lives. (Leaving them in open bags lets the flavours escape and mingle; you'll end up with a gently scented cupboard and everything tasting of cumin.) Although supermarkets now stock an impressive range of blends and individual spices, we often buy ours in Asian grocers, where you can get big bags of quality spices for a fraction of the cost. Wherever you buy them, choose packs from the gloomy back of the shelf, where the light won't have done any damage. Whole spices keep longer than powders – and taste better when freshly ground (even better when toasted and freshly ground).

CHILLIES

In the UK, the medium-sized chillies we buy in supermarkets can be very mild at certain times of the year. Look out for smaller, hotter chillies, such as bird's-eye or finger chillies. It's not always the case, but little chillies are very often more fiery, with the exception of large frilly-looking Scotch bonnets, which are mouth-numbingly sour and hot. Older, riper chillies tend to be hotter, so if you leave them in the fridge for a while, your mild-mannered supermarket chillies may turn feisty. Green chillies have a more bitter, vegetal flavour, while red ones tend to be sweeter, and sometimes hotter too.

Always taste a little piece of a chilli before adding it to a dish (except for the searingly hot beasts, like Scotch bonnets) – once you've added it, you can't take the heat out, but you can always add more later, if you like. When deseeding a chilli, to make it milder, remember to remove the white pith, too, as that's actually where the worst of the heat is hiding.

HEALTH

Spices have been used in traditional medicine all over the world for millennia, and gradually more formal research is being done to discover their powers. Turmeric and ginger are thought to be anti-inflammatory (turmeric may be antiviral, antibacterial and antifungal, too); cinnamon is considered an antioxidant and may promote heart health; cayenne and chillies may kick-start the metabolism; fenugreek may help to regulate blood sugar; and, in some alternative medicine practices, cardamom is used to remove toxins from the body.

VEG IT UP

We want our books to be friendly to anyone who chooses to eat fewer or no animal products. In many of our recipes, you can swap the meat, fish or dairy for vegetables, pulses, tofu or a ready-made meat replacement.

Canned unripe green jackfruit, rinsed, shredded and with the tougher core removed, is a startlingly good substitute for chicken. So is light seitan, a wheat-based meat replacement that has been used for centuries in Chinese cooking (if you've ever tried mock duck, you've eaten seitan). Dark seitan has a beefier flavour, so can be used instead of red meat. Both are best sliced and browned first, then added to a curry when it's almost ready to serve.

Firm tofu works well instead of salmon or cod in fish curries – just submerge it in the broth in the same way as you would fish, or chop and fry it first to lightly brown. Although we love soft, silky tofu, we tend not to use it in curries, as it can too easily fall apart.

Vegetarians can swap paneer, an Indian cheese, into most meat curries – treat it as we do on page 60, then add towards the end of cooking.

Crunchy vegetables, such as cauliflower, carrot and peppers, work well in many curries, as do sweet potatoes, aubergines and mushrooms – whether to cook them first depends on how long the curry needs to cook. You can extend meat dishes like keema (see page 145) by adding cooked pulses, such as Puy or black lentils, or use canned chickpeas or black beans in saucier curries.

Crisp green vegetables, when in season, are excellent in soupy curries – go for long thin spears of broccoli, green beans, snap peas, asparagus, sliced kale, sweetheart or hispi cabbage, or slices of courgette.

MILD

CURRY UDON NOODLES

SERVES 2

PREP TIME: 15 MINS • COOK TIME: 30 MINS

NF

2 **eggs**

250g **extra-firm plain tofu**, cut into 1 x 3cm fingers

2 teaspoons **neutral cooking oil**

1 small **onion**, halved and finely sliced

150g **shiitake mushrooms**, sliced

2 tablespoons **butter**

2 heaped tablespoons **plain flour**

1 tablespoon **mild Indian curry powder**

1 teaspoon **garam masala**

600ml hot **dashi stock** (or mix 1 teaspoon **soy sauce**, 1 teaspoon **fish sauce** and 2 teaspoons **vegetable bouillon powder** with 600ml **hot water**)

150g **dried udon noodles**

soy sauce, to taste

2 **spring onions**, finely sliced on a diagonal

1–2 generous pinches of **shichimi togarashi seasoning**, to garnish (optional) (to make your own, combine 1 pinch each of some or all of the following: **sesame seeds**, **black pepper**, **Szechuan pepper**, **ground ginger**, **seaweed flakes** or **powder**, **red pepper flakes** or crumbled **dried chillies**, **garlic powder**)

salt, to taste

This curry made its way to Japan from India via the British, which is why it is made with curry powder. It's a gentle, soothing curry, with thick noodles and a Japanese sesame-and-spice seasoning, shichimi togarashi.

Place the eggs in a steamer basket set over a pan of simmering water. Steam for 8 minutes, for soft-yolked, hard-boiled eggs. Cool under running cold water, then set aside.

Press the tofu between two sheets of kitchen paper to squeeze out the moisture. Set a wide deep pan over a medium heat and add the oil. When hot, add the tofu and cook until golden and no longer sticking to the pan. Turn each piece and cook until golden again. Remove from the pan and set aside. Add the onions and mushrooms to the pan and sauté for about 5 minutes, until the onion is beginning to soften.

Turn the heat to low and add the butter. When melted, add the flour and cook, stirring, for 3–4 minutes, until combined into a smooth golden roux. Mix in the curry powder and garam masala and cook for a further 2 minutes.

Next, add a little of the hot stock. Mix until smooth, then gradually add the rest. Bring up to a simmer, and cook, stirring, until the broth has thickened slightly.

Add the noodles to the pan and cook according to the packet instructions, stirring often so they don't clump together. Meanwhile, peel and halve the eggs.

Taste the broth for salt and umami, and add a pinch of salt or dash of soy sauce, as needed. Divide the curry udon between two bowls, decorate with the halved eggs, and sprinkle with the spring onions and shichimi togarashi, if using.

≡ **TIP** ≡

Vegans can leave out the eggs and add
vegetables, such as Asian greens and thinly
sliced carrots or beans. You can also buy
ready-made Japanese curry roux.

1960s CHICKEN TIKKA MASALA

SERVES 4

PREP TIME: 25 MINS • MARINATING TIME: 1–24 HOURS • COOK TIME: 45 MINS

NF • SoF

FOR THE MARINADE:

2 tablespoons freshly squeezed **lemon juice**

2 tablespoons **full-fat plain yoghurt**

2cm piece of **ginger**, finely grated

1 clove of **garlic**, crushed

¼ teaspoon **hot chilli powder**

½ teaspoon **sweet smoked paprika**

salt and **freshly ground black pepper**

FOR THE CURRY:

1 tablespoon **neutral cooking oil**

800g **skinless chicken breast**, cut into rough 3cm chunks

3 **onions**, finely chopped

4 cloves of **garlic**, crushed

4cm piece of **ginger**, finely grated

2 teaspoons **tomato purée**

seeds from 4 **green cardamom pods**, ground in a pestle and mortar

1 teaspoon **ground coriander**

2 teaspoons **paprika**

1 teaspoon **sweet smoked paprika**

½ teaspoon **ground cinnamon**

1 teaspoon **ground cumin**

2 teaspoons **garam masala**

Chicken tikka, peshwari naan, poppadoms and mango chutney made up the first Indian meal John ever ate, in a tandoori house opposite the Old Bailey in London, aged 14. After growing up on spaghetti bolognaise and shepherd's pie, it was revelatory.

Is tikka masala from Glasgow? Or the Punjab? Or Delhi? Was it invented by a Bangladeshi chef in London in the 1960s? Or did the original recipe involve cream of tomato soup, because a Scottish bus driver sent back a plate of chicken tikka he thought was too dry? There are so many stories – and no one knows for sure – but it is one of the most popular curries in Britain and has been for decades. We'd like to thank Madhur Jaffrey and Felicity Cloake – both their recipes played a part in the creation of this one.

You can use this recipe to make a vegetarian or vegan version of tikka masala. Simply substitute the meat with extra-firm tofu or cauliflower, courgette or peppers, and use non-dairy full-fat yoghurt (coconut or soy work well) in place of both the dairy yoghurt and cream. Fish eaters can use firm fish such as salmon, but cut the marinating time to 15 minutes.

Mix all the marinade ingredients together in a bowl and season well with salt and pepper. Use your hands to work the marinade into the chicken, then cover and chill in the fridge for 1–24 hours.

Heat the oil in a large heavy-based saucepan over a medium heat, add the onions and gently sauté until soft and beginning to brown, about 8 minutes. Add the garlic, ginger and tomato purée and cook for a further 3–4 minutes, stirring often.

¼–½ teaspoon **hot chilli powder**, to taste

400g **chopped tomatoes** or **passata**

600ml **water**

3–5 tablespoons **single cream**

a big handful of **fresh coriander leaves**

warm **Naan** (see page 198), to serve

salt and **freshly ground black pepper**

Add the ground cardamom seeds, ground coriander, paprika, smoked paprika, cinnamon, cumin, garam masala, chilli powder and chopped tomatoes or passata to the pan. Cook, stirring and squashing the tomatoes, for about 10 minutes, until the sauce is really thick. Add the water, a generous pinch of salt and some freshly ground black pepper and bring up to a simmer. Cook for about 15 minutes, until the sauce has reduced – it shouldn't be wet, so continue to reduce if necessary.

Meanwhile, heat the grill to its highest setting. Remove the chicken from the marinade, but don't scrape it off. You can thread the meat onto skewers or cook it resting on the grill pan rack (lined with foil for easier cleaning up). Place the meat under the hot grill, about 10cm away from the heat, and cook for about 8 minutes on each side, until just charred on the edges.

While the chicken is cooking, remove the sauce from the heat and add 3 tablespoons of the cream. Taste and add more if wished – it should be creamy, but not overwhelmingly so. Carefully purée the sauce in a blender or food processor until smooth. Work in batches if necessary, as some blenders may explode if overfilled with hot liquid. Transfer the sauce back to the pan and keep warm.

When the chicken is ready, stir it into the sauce and cook for a further 5 minutes. Remove from the heat and stir through half of the coriander leaves. Serve, scattered with the remaining coriander, with naan breads (and three or four other indulgent curries...).

== TIP ==

You can also cook the meat over a barbecue. Wait until the coals are white, with no flames, and cook the meat at least 20cm above the coals, so that the chicken cooks through before the marinade burns.

═ TIP ═

To make your own Vietnamese curry powder, place the following ingredients in a pestle and mortar or spice grinder and grind to a powder: 5 cloves, ½ teaspoon fennel seeds, ½ teaspoon coriander seeds, 1 teaspoon cumin seeds, scant ½ teaspoon hot chilli powder, a generous pinch of ground nutmeg, 1 teaspoon ground turmeric, a pinch of ground mace and a pinch of ground cinnamon.

'CA RI GA' VIETNAMESE CHICKEN CURRY

SERVES 4

PREP TIME: 25 MINS • COOK TIME: 1 HOUR

WF • GF (check fish sauce ingredients and serve with rice) • DF • NF • SoF

1 tablespoon **neutral cooking oil**

1 **onion**, finely sliced

4–8 (depending on size) skin-on, bone-in **chicken thighs**, cut into 2 or 3 pieces

1 tablespoon **Vietnamese curry powder** (ready-made or see tip)

4 cloves of **garlic**, crushed

2 tablespoons **tomato purée**

200g (1 small) **sweet potato**, peeled and cut into chunks

200g **potatoes**, cut into chunks

150g (1 large) **carrot**, peeled, halved and cut into 1cm pieces

3cm piece of **ginger**, peeled and cut into 3 long pieces

1 stick of **lemongrass**, bruised

1 **bay leaf**

1 tablespoon **fish sauce**, plus extra

a generous pinch of **sugar**

200ml **full-fat coconut milk**, from the top of an unshaken can

freshly squeezed **lemon juice**, to taste

4 sprigs **Thai basil**

salt

2 big handfuls of **fresh coriander leaves**

4 **spring onions**, finely chopped

baguettes or **steamed rice**, to serve

This is our version of a classic soupy Vietnamese chicken and root vegetable curry, which is often served with the Vietnamese version of a French baguette, adopted during the French colonial era.

Thanks to food blogger Ginger and Scotch for turning us on to the power of homemade Vietnamese curry powder – our recipe is loosely based on hers. You can buy it ready-made online and in Asian food stores (we like Vianco Bot Cary) or use mild Madras curry powder.

Heat the oil in a large heavy-based pan with a lid over a high heat. Add the onion and chicken thighs and soften the onions while browning the chicken to a light golden brown. Work in batches, if necesssary. Return all the browned meat to the pan and add the curry powder, garlic and tomato purée and cook, stirring, for about 3 minutes.

Add the vegetables, ginger, lemongrass, bay leaf, fish sauce, sugar and enough hot water to cover (600–800ml). Cover with a lid and bring up to a gentle simmer, then turn the heat to low and cook for 30 minutes.

Remove the lid, add the coconut milk and bring back to a simmer. Cook, uncovered, for a further 10 minutes, until the chicken is cooked through and the vegetables are tender. Remove and discard the lemongrass and ginger.

Remove from the heat and add a generous squeeze of lemon and the Thai basil. Stir, then taste and add more fish sauce or salt, or lemon juice, if needed. Divide between wide bowls and scatter over the coriander leaves and spring onions.

Serve with hunks of baguette, or steamed rice.

MASSAMAN CURRY

SERVES 4
PREP TIME: 25 MINS • COOK TIME: 2½ HOURS
WF • GF • DF • SoF

FOR THE PASTE:
½ teaspoon **coriander seeds**
½ teaspoon **cumin seeds**
4 **cloves**
seeds from 5 **green cardamom pods**
¼ teaspoon **ground cinnamon**
½ teaspoon **dried red chilli flakes**
¼ teaspoon **ground mace**
a pinch of **freshly grated nutmeg**
freshly ground black pepper
1 teaspoon **galangal paste**
1 **shallot**, very finely chopped
1 stick of **lemongrass**, outer layer
    removed, very finely chopped
3 cloves of **garlic**, crushed
1 teaspoon **fish sauce**

FOR THE CURRY:
400ml can **full-fat coconut milk**, unshaken
650g **braising beef**, cut into small chunks
350g **potatoes**, cut into small chunks
½ a small **onion**, finely sliced
6 **lime leaves**
fish sauce, to taste
tamarind paste or **concentrate**, to taste
unsalted peanuts or **cashews**, to serve
sticky rice, to serve

Rebecca was completely bewildered when she arrived in Bangkok for the first time when she was nineteen – everything seemed extraordinary. But on her first night in a backpackers' hostel, she had this mellow curry for dinner and all was well with the world. Massaman is different to most other Thai curries – there are no fiery chillies. The curry base works with chicken, fish or veg – just reduce the cooking time accordingly and only add water as needed, rather than the full amount.

For the paste, place all the dry spices and a generous grinding of black pepper in a pestle and mortar and grind to a powder. Add the galangal paste, shallot, lemongrass and garlic and pound to a very smooth paste. Stir in the fish sauce.

Spoon a dollop of the thick cream from the top of the coconut milk can into a large heavy-based pan with a lid, set over a medium heat. Let it melt and begin to sizzle, then add the paste (or 3 tablespoons of ready-made curry paste) and fry for 3–4 minutes, until fragrant. When the paste develops an oily sheen, add the remaining coconut milk and 200ml hot water and bring gently up to a simmer. Add the beef, then partially cover and simmer on the lowest possible heat for 1½–2 hours, or until the beef is tender. Keep an eye on liquid levels – the sauce needs to reduce and thicken a little, but should never become dry or sticky, so add splashes of water when needed.

Add the potatoes and onion, plus a little water if there isn't enough liquid to cover, and bring back to a simmer. Cook for 12–15 minutes, or until the potatoes are tender but not falling apart. Towards the end of cooking, add the lime leaves and 1 teaspoon each of fish sauce and tamarind paste. Taste, adding more of each until you're happy with the balance of sour and salt. Add the nuts and serve with the rice.

≡ TIP ≡

To turn this into
a Korean-style curry
dish, serve some kimchi
(a fermented cabbage
condiment) alongside.

THÉRÈSE'S CHICKEN KATSU AND CURRY SAUCE

SERVES 4
PREP TIME: 25 MINS • COOK TIME: 40 MINS
NF

4 skinless, boneless **chicken thighs**

150g **plain flour**

2 **eggs**, beaten

400g **panko breadcrumbs**

2 tablespoons **cooking oil**

salt and **freshly ground black pepper**

steamed rice, to serve

FOR THE SAUCE:

1½ tablespoons **neutral cooking oil**

1 **onion**, finely chopped

100g (1 medium) **carrot**, finely diced

2 cloves of **garlic**, finely chopped

½ teaspoon **ground cumin**

1 tablespoon **Madras curry powder**

1 teaspoon **ground turmeric**

200ml **chicken stock**

1½ tablespoons **soy sauce**

2 teaspoons **honey** (or more, to taste)

1 tablespoon **cornflour** mixed into a
   smooth paste with 2 tablespoons **water**

2 tablespoons **single cream**

1 teaspoon **garam masala**

salt and **freshly ground black pepper**

We asked LEON's Instagram followers for their best curry recipes and the winners got the chance to have their recipe in this book. We loved Thérèse Gaughan's take on Japanese chicken katsu. For more of her recipes, check out her website: www.kitchenexile.com.

To make the sauce, heat the oil in a saucepan over a low heat, add the onion, carrot and garlic and fry for 10–15 minutes, stirring, until softened. Add the cumin, curry powder and turmeric and cook, stirring often, for 5 minutes. Stir in the stock, soy sauce and honey and cook for a further 10 minutes. Add the cornflour paste and the cream and cook, stirring, until it starts to thicken (add up to 50ml water if it gets too thick). Add the garam masala and season to taste with salt and pepper (add a little more honey, if you prefer it sweet). Keep warm.

Lay the chicken thighs on a chopping board, cover with clingfilm and bash with a rolling pin to 1cm thick. If this makes the pieces very large, cut in half. Place the flour on a plate and season. Place the eggs into a wide bowl and the breadcrumbs on a separate plate. Dip the chicken pieces first into the flour, then the egg and finally into the breadcrumbs, ensuring they are well coated.

Heat the oil in a frying pan over a low heat. When hot, fry the chicken for 7–10 minutes, turning every 3 minutes, until cooked through. Drain on kitchen paper. (You may need to work in batches. Wipe out the pan and start each batch with fresh oil.)

Slice the katsu chicken into 2cm strips and serve with the sauce and rice.

EVERYDAY DHAL

SERVES 4 WITH LEFTOVERS
PREP TIME: 10 MINS • COOK TIME: 55 MINS
WF • GF • DF • V • Ve • NF • SoF • SUITABLE FOR FREEZING

200g **yellow split peas**, picked over
  and rinsed

200g **split red lentils**

3 tablespoons **neutral cooking oil**

1 **onion**, finely chopped

3 cloves of **garlic**, crushed or finely grated

3cm piece of **ginger**, peeled and
  finely grated

2 teaspoons **black mustard seeds**

1 teaspoon **ground turmeric**

1 teaspoon **cumin seeds**

1 teaspoon **ground coriander**

½ teaspoon **garam masala**

1–3 teaspoons finely chopped
  red chilli, to taste

½–1 teaspoons **dried red chilli flakes**

a squeeze of **lime** or **lemon juice**

salt and **freshly ground black pepper**

a handful of **fresh coriander**, to garnish

TO SERVE:

Parathas (see pages 205–6)

plain yoghurt or **Raita** (see pages 163–4)

spicy chutney or **Lime Pickle** (see page 214)

Dhal is an Indian staple, a lentil-based curry that can be as soupy or as thick as you like. We can't get enough and batch-cook it so we always have a portion (or 10) in the freezer. Eat with flatbreads, pickles and yoghurt.

Place the yellow split peas and 1 litre of water in a large deep pan with a lid and bring up to a fast boil. Use a large spoon to skim off and discard any scum that rises to the surface. Turn the heat down to a simmer, cover and cook for 30 minutes.

Add the red lentils to the pan along with another 1 litre of water, cover and cook for a further 20 minutes, or until the red lentils are soft and collapsing into the broth.

Meanwhile, make the temper mixture. Add 1 tablespoon of the oil to a frying pan set over a medium heat. Add the onion and cook for 12–15 minutes, stirring often, until caramelized and brown. Add the garlic and ginger and cook for 2–3 minutes, then add the remaining oil and the mustard seeds. When they begin to pop, add the rest of the spices, the fresh chilli and dried chilli flakes and a generous pinch of black pepper. Cook until the spices are fragrant but not scorched.

When the split peas are soft and the lentils have collapsed, remove the dhal pan from the heat. Pour in the hot temper mixture, including the oil, and stir. Add some salt, then taste and add more as needed (you can also add more hot water, if you like a soupier dhal). Just before serving, squeeze in a little fresh lemon or lime juice, and stir again.

Serve garnished with a little fresh coriander and eat hot, with parathas, plain yoghurt or raita and spicy chutney or pickles.

≡ TIP ≡

You can do so much with dhal: add shredded spinach, chopped tomatoes, cauliflower florets or finely diced potato to the pan, and cook in the dhal. Flavour with curry leaves, bay leaves or cardamom.

LIPU'S BENGALI FISH TENGA

2–3 tablespoons **neutral cooking oil**

1 medium **onion**, finely sliced

a pinch of **salt**

3 cloves of **garlic**, finely sliced

¼ teaspoon **ground turmeric**

400g **canned chopped tomatoes** or chopped **fresh tomatoes**

500g firm-fleshed **fish**, such as **trout**, **salmon**, **turbot** or **monkfish** (ideally bone-in) in large pieces

400ml **freshly boiled water**

TO SERVE:

a handful of **fresh coriander**

2–3 finely sliced **green chillies**

plain rice

Lipu is mum to Shumi, a very good friend of LEON: 'This is Bengal's answer to France's bouillabaisse. An astringent, soothing broth made with tomatoes and fresh herbs, it is usually eaten at the end of a meal as a palate cleanser. It can be made vegan by swapping out the fish for sliced courgette or marrow, cucumbers or even unripe melon.'

Heat 2 tablespoons of the oil in a heavy-based saucepan with a lid over a medium-low heat. When hot, add the onion and salt and cook until soft and translucent. Add the garlic and continue to cook, until the garlic starts to colour a little, then add the ground turmeric and cook until fragrant and the oil separates from the onions.

Add the tomatoes and continue to cook until the tomatoes and onions have completely broken down, adding the final tablespoon of oil if needed. Add the fish and cook for 1–2 minutes, gently stirring to coat it in the onion and spice mixture.

Add the hot water and bring up to a simmer without stirring. Cover with a lid, reduce the heat to low and cook for 5–10 minutes, or until the fish is opaque and easily flakes apart or falls off the bone.

Garnish with fresh coriander and fresh green chillies and serve with plain rice.

=TIP=

You could use raw scallops, prawns or diced aubergines for this dish; just simmer until cooked through.

CARIBBEAN CHICKEN & MANGO CURRY

SERVES 4
PREP TIME: 25 MINS • COOK TIME: 50 MINS
WF • GF • DF • NF • SoF

2 tablespoons **neutral cooking oil**

1 **onion**, finely diced

1 clove of **garlic**, crushed

a pinch of **salt**

3cm piece of **ginger**, peeled and finely grated

1 **carrot**, finely diced

1 teaspoon **tomato purée**

2 teaspoons **hot** or **mild Jamaican curry powder** (make mild curry powder hotter by adding ¼ teaspoon **hot chilli powder**)

600g skinless, boneless **chicken thighs** or **breasts**, cut into bite-sized pieces

200ml hot **chicken stock**

1 **Scotch bonnet chilli**, left whole, or 2 **hot red chillies**, slit down one side

3 sprigs **thyme**

1 medium **potato**, peeled and cut into 2cm cubes

400ml **full-fat coconut milk**, from a well-shaken can

½–1 **mango** (depending on size and sweetness), peeled and cut into 2cm pieces

Coconut Rice 'n' Peas (see page 178) or **plain rice**, to serve

Make this as hot as you can handle by using a Scotch bonnet chilli – the coconut and mango smooth out this curry's fiery edges.

Heat the oil in a large deep saucepan with a lid, set over a medium heat. Add the onion and cook for about 8 minutes, until beginning to soften and brown. Add a generous pinch of salt along with the garlic, ginger, carrot and tomato purée and cook for 1 minute, stirring, then add the curry powder. Cook, stirring all the time, for 2 minutes, then add the chicken and sauté for 4 minutes, thoroughly coating it in the spice mixture.

Pour the stock into the pan, add the chilli, thyme and potato and bring up to a simmer. Cover and cook until the chicken is cooked through and the potato is tender, about 20–25 minutes. Pour in the coconut milk and add the mango pieces, then stir well and bring back to a simmer.

Taste for salt and spice and remove the chillies if it is fiery enough for you, or add a pinch of hot chilli powder if not. Remove the chillies and thyme sprigs before serving. Serve with coconut rice and peas, or plain rice.

═ TIP ═

This is also good with lamb – add it with the chillies and thyme but, since it will take 1½–2 hours to become tender, add a little more liquid and wait until the last 25 minutes to add the potatoes.

COLOMBO DE MARTINIQUE

SERVES 4

PREP TIME: 20 MINS • COOK TIME: 53 MINS

WF • GF • DF • NF • SoF (check stock)

2 tablespoons **neutral cooking oil**

1 **onion**, finely diced

1 **red pepper**, deseeded and chopped into 1cm pieces

2 cloves of **garlic**, crushed

2 teaspoons **hot** or **mild Caribbean/Jamaican curry powder** + ¼ teaspoon **ground cloves**, or 2¼ teaspoons **Colombo curry powder**

600g boneless, skinless **chicken thighs** or **breasts**, cut into chunks

400ml hot **chicken** or **vegetable stock**

2 medium **potatoes**, peeled and diced

1 **bay leaf**

3 sprigs **thyme**

2 sprigs **flat-leaf parsley**

1 **Scotch bonnet chilli**, left whole, or 2 **hot green** or **red chillies**, slit down one side

a generous pinch of **salt**

1 **courgette**, cut into rough 2cm pieces

2 teaspoons freshly squeezed **lime juice**, to serve

steamed rice, to serve

This recipe comes from the French Caribbean, but is thought to have originated in Sri Lanka. Colombo curry powder is very similar to other more readily available Caribbean curry powders, except it contains cloves, so we mix the two together.

Heat the oil in a large deep saucepan set over a medium heat, add the onion and cook for about 8 minutes, until beginning to soften and brown. Add the red pepper and garlic and cook for 1 minute, then add the curry powder and ground cloves, if needed, and cook for 1 minute, stirring. Add the chicken and sauté for 3–4 minutes, thoroughly coating it in the spice mixture.

Add the stock, potatoes, bay leaf, thyme, parsley and chilli, along with a good pinch of salt. Bring up to a simmer and cook for 25 minutes (if the pan seems dry, add more water). When the chicken is tender, add the courgette and cook for 6–8 minutes, until tender but not mushy.

Remove from the heat and taste for salt. Remove and discard the whole chillies, parsley and thyme sprigs and bay leaf. Squeeze over the lime juice and stir through. Go carefully as the lime shouldn't be overwhelming.

Serve with steamed rice.

═ TIP ═

Sometimes, Colombo is made with coconut milk rather than stock, or a 50:50 mix of the two.

CAPE MALAY CURRIED BEEF

SERVES 4
PREP TIME: 20 MINS • COOK TIME: 3½ HOURS
WF • GF • DF • NF • SoF (check rotis) **• SUITABLE FOR FREEZING**

1 tablespoon **neutral cooking oil**

800g **stewing beef**, diced and patted dry with kitchen paper

2 **onions**, finely chopped

5 cloves of **garlic**, crushed

4cm piece of **ginger**, peeled and finely grated

3 **hot red chillies** (deseeded or not, to taste), finely chopped

1 **red pepper**, deseeded and diced

2 tablespoons **tomato purée**

700ml **hot water**, or more as needed

1 tablespoon **apple cider vinegar**

2 **bay leaves**

3cm stick of **cinnamon**

6 **green cardamom pods**

2 sprigs **thyme**

75g **dried apricots**, chopped

salt and **freshly ground black pepper**

fresh coriander, to garnish (optional)

rotis or **plain rice**, to serve

This is often cooked with cubed potatoes added for the last half hour of cooking.

This is a South African curry with a long and sorrowful history. It was created by slave communities, made up of people brought to the Cape from Malaysia and across Asia. Part stew, part curry, the signature feature of a Cape Malay curry is its sweet sharpness, alongside warming spices such as cinnamon.

Heat the oil in a large, deep, heavy-based pan with a tight-fitting lid over a high heat. Add the beef and sear briskly until brown all over, stirring continuously. Remove from the pan with a slotted spoon and set aside.

Add the onions to the pan, reduce the heat to medium and cook until nicely browned and softened, about 10–15 minutes (test a piece of onion with a spoon – it shouldn't be firm). If the juices seem to be catching, reduce the heat to low, add 1–2 tablespoons of water and let it bubble away to deglaze the pan.

Add the garlic, ginger, red chillies and red pepper and cook for 2–3 minutes, stirring. Add the tomato purée and cook, stirring, for a further 2 minutes. Return the meat to the pan and add the water, vinegar, bay leaves, cinnamon stick, green cardamom pods and thyme. Season then cover with the lid and cook on the lowest possible heat for 1 hour.

Remove and discard the cinnamon, add the chopped dried apricots and top up the liquid with more hot water, if needed. Continue to cook, stirring every 30 minutes, for a further 2 hours, or until the meat is melting into the curry sauce.

Remove the bay leaves and thyme sprigs before serving. Taste and add more salt, if needed. Serve garnished with coriander leaves, with rotis or rice.

FIERY

HEARTBREAK CURRY

SERVES 4
PREP TIME: 20 MINS (PLUS OPTIONAL 2 HOURS MARINATING) • COOK TIME: AT LEAST 1¾ HOURS
WF • GF • DF • NF • SoF (check stock) • SUITABLE FOR FREEZING

1 tablespoon **mild curry powder** (ideally Jamaican)

750g (1kg if bone-in) **goat**, **lamb** or **mutton**, trimmed and cut into chunks

1 large **onion**, finely sliced

1 tablespoon **neutral cooking oil**

2 teaspoons **tomato purée**

50g **tomatoes**, deseeded and finely chopped

4 sprigs **thyme**

1 very hot **Scotch bonnet chilli**, whole with a small slit cut into it (handle with care)

4 **allspice berries**

1 **red pepper**, deseeded and cut into small chunks

2 cloves of **garlic**, crushed

500ml hot **chicken** or **vegetable stock**

250g **waxy** or **new potatoes**, cut into small chunks

2 **spring onions**, roughly chopped

salt and **freshly ground black pepper**

Coconut Rice 'n' Peas (see page 178), to serve

Rebecca Di Mambro, who works in the marketing team at LEON, reckons this Caribbean curried goat is so hot it counts as a heartbreak curry – that is, the perfect post-breakup curry. 'What? I'm not crying. It's just that this curry is terribly spicy.'

*Goat is a fairly sustainable meat, so it's worth seeking out online or in Caribbean food stores, but you can use lamb or mutton instead. We also created a plantain version of this in our **Fast Vegan** book – look out for fruit with a good covering of brown spots, peel and slice into 1cm chunks, then simmer in the curry for an hour or until tender.*

Combine the curry powder, meat and onion in a large bowl and use your hands to rub the curry powder in well. It can be marinated for a few hours in the fridge, if you have time, or you can cook straight away.

Heat the oil in a large heavy-based pan with a lid over a medium heat. When shimmering hot, add the meat and onions and any leftover curry powder, mix well so that it is well coated in oil, then cover with the lid. Cook for 4–5 minutes, then stir and re-cover. Repeat, stirring every couple of minutes, for a further 10 minutes, until the mixture is slightly browned and the meat is releasing juices into the pan.

Add the tomato purée and cook for 3 minutes, stirring, then add the tomatoes, thyme, Scotch bonnet chilli, allspice berries, red pepper and garlic, and cook, gently stirring, for a further 3 minutes. Add the stock and bring up to a simmer, then cover with the lid, reduce the heat to low and cook for 1 hour.

After this time, taste the broth – if the chilli has already given it plenty of lip-tingling sour heat, remove and discard it. If not, leave it in (but be warned, it may fall apart and disappear into the curry!). Add a little salt and pepper, if needed (some Jamaican curry powders already contain both). If the meat feels as though it is almost done – and it probably won't just yet, but it's important to check the heat levels at this point – stir in the potatoes and spring onions, re-cover and cook for a final 30 minutes. If the meat still feels very firm, continue to cook the curry, covered, for an hour or even longer, tasting the meat before adding the potatoes and spring onions. When the time is up the potatoes should be tender and the meat falling apart.

Serve with coconut rice 'n' peas.

TIP

How long the meat will take to cook can vary quite a bit, depending on the cut of meat and the age of the animal, as well as whether you use goat or lamb. Bone-in cuts may take even longer than stated here. This is one for cooking when you have plenty of time, and won't come to harm being left to simmer on low for hours, as long as you keep the liquid levels topped up.

≡ **TIP** ≡

Pork is commonly served
in red curry in Thailand, but you
can use vegetables, fish, seafood
or chicken, if you prefer. The crushed
dried red chillies can be substituted
with Thai dried mild red spur chillies,
in which case use double or even
triple the amount, to taste.

THAI RED CURRY WITH CRISPY PORK BELLY

SERVES 4
PREP TIME: 25 MINS • COOK TIME: 30 MINS
WF • GF • DF • NF • SoF

650g **pork belly**, cut into 3cm chunks

a generous pinch of **fine salt**

vegetable oil, for frying

400ml **full-fat coconut milk**

150g **long green beans**, trimmed and sliced into 3cm pieces

leaves from 2 sprigs **Thai basil**, to garnish

4 **lime wedges**, to serve

sticky rice, to serve

FOR THE CURRY PASTE:

6 **lime leaves**, finely chopped

1 **red chilli** (deseeded or not, to taste)

1 clove of **garlic**, finely chopped

1 **shallot**, finely chopped

1 teaspoon **galangal paste**

2 teaspoons **fish sauce**

½ teaspoon **ground cumin**

½ teaspoon **ground coriander**

a generous grinding of **black pepper**

1 stick of **lemongrass**, peeled, base trimmed and finely diced

½ teaspoon **dried red chillies**, to taste

1 tablespoon **very finely chopped coriander root** or stalks (optional)

Often, pork belly is brined, simmered and then roasted for a crispy result, so this is a total cheat – we just deep-fry it in little nuggets, then plunge it into the red curry at the last minute, for maximum crunch.

Sprinkle the salt over the pork and set aside for 10–15 minutes.

Pour about 3cm of oil into a deep, high-sided pan and heat until it reaches 180°C or until a cube of bread browns in 30 seconds .

Pat the pork dry with kitchen paper. Using tongs, add 3 or 4 chunks of pork at a time to the hot oil (if you have a splatter guard for your pan, use it). Fry for 5–7 minutes, turning once or twice, until golden and crispy. Remove to drain on kitchen paper and keep warm.

Use a pestle and mortar, blender or spice grinder to blitz all the paste ingredients until smooth – the best way is in a pestle and mortar but this will take a while.

Heat 1 tablespoon of vegetable oil in a large heavy-based saucepan over a low heat, add the spice paste and cook for 3–4 minutes, until fragrant. Add about two-thirds of the coconut milk and slowly increase the heat to bring to a simmer (don't rush or the coconut milk may split). Add the remaining coconut milk and the beans and cook until the beans are just tender, about 4–5 minutes.

Taste for salt or chilli heat and adjust if needed. Just before serving, add the pork to heat through, but do this as late as you can or it will lose its crunch. Garnish with Thai basil leaves and serve with lime wedges and sticky rice.

GREEN CURRY AKA GAP YEAR CURRY

SERVES 4
PREP TIME: 20–25 MINS • COOK TIME: UP TO 30 MINS
WF • GF • DF • V • Ve (if using seaweed powder or salt) • NF • SoF (if not using tofu, seitan, mock duck)

2 x 400ml cans **full-fat coconut milk** (at least 60% coconut), unshaken

8 **lime leaves**

300g **mixed vegetables** (choose from **Thai aubergines**, **purple aubergine**, **sweet potato**, **squash** of any kind, sliced **greens**, **baby corn**, **long green beans**, shredded **canned unripe green jackfruit**, thinly sliced **canned bamboo shoots**, **peppers**, **mangetout** or **snap peas**), cut into bite-sized pieces, as necessary

650g **protein** (choose from **boneless chicken**, **steak**, **fish**, **seafood**, **browned tofu**, **browned seitan/wheat meat** or **vegan mock duck**), cut into bite-sized pieces or strips, as necessary

up to 100ml **hot water**

leaves from 2–3 sprigs of **Thai basil**

1 **red chilli**, thinly sliced on an angle

extra **fish sauce** or **salt**, to taste

Thai jasmine rice, to serve

FOR THE CURRY PASTE (MAKES ABOUT 4 TABLESPOONS):

4 medium **green chillies**, very finely chopped

The famous Thai green curry gets its colour from the green chillies in its freshly made paste – not from herbs, as many people think. You can use 3–4 tablespoons of good-quality ready-made curry paste instead, if you prefer. Add whatever mix of protein and vegetables you fancy.

Green curry and other Thai dishes have made regular appearances on the LEON menu over the years – they are a favourite with John and his family (see page 47). We find the mixture of creamy coconut, salty, hot, sour and almost sweet curry sauce to be irresistible, and this recipe has become a bit of a weeknight regular, especially since you can make it meaty, fishy or plant-based.

Make the paste in either a pestle and mortar or small blender, although the best results do come from pounding it by hand. We often cheat and blitz it first and then finish off with the pestle and mortar to really get the flavours to blossom. Either way, pound the paste ingredients to a smooth paste and look for the oils to be released.

Spoon 1 tablespoon of the thick cream from the top of one of the coconut milk cans into a large deep pan, set over a medium heat. Let it melt and begin to sizzle, then add the paste and fry for at least 5 minutes, or until the bright green oil is released and the paste thickens rather than looking wet. Once it smells fragrant, add the remaining coconut milk and the lime leaves and gently bring to a simmer. You will see dots of green oil on the surface – a good thing.

RECIPE CONTINUES ⟶

3 **shallots**, very finely chopped

4 cloves of **garlic**, crushed

1½ teaspoons **galangal paste**

1 stick of **lemongrass**, outer layer removed, very finely chopped

½ teaspoon **ground coriander**

½ teaspoon **ground cumin**

2 tablespoons very finely chopped **coriander root** or **stalks**

1 teaspoon **fish sauce** or ½ teaspoon **Thai shrimp paste** (or **seaweed powder**)

freshly ground black pepper, to taste

If adding vegetables that need more cooking than your chosen protein (such as butternut squash), add them now and cook until just tender, before adding the protein. Chicken pieces will need about 20 minutes, but salmon, tofu and crisp vegetables like green beans will only need a few minutes in the broth. If you find there isn't enough liquid to cover everything in the pan, add the water and bring back to a simmer.

Once everything is cooked to your liking, remove from the heat and add the Thai basil leaves and red chilli. Taste the broth and add more fish sauce or salt, as needed (depending on how salty your fish sauce is, if using, you might need up to 2 more teaspoons).

Serve with Thai jasmine rice.

=≡ TIP =≡

You can cook bone-in chicken in this (or even a whole chicken, chopped into small pieces), but poach in boiling water for about 20 minutes before placing it in the curry, and use its cooking liquid instead of the hot water.

JOHN'S THAI FOOD DISCOVERY

'The first Thai food I ever ate was at university. A basement café opened up opposite my halls of residence, and it was probably the only Thai restaurant in town, way back in 1993. I don't think younger people necessarily realize how scarce Asian food was then – it wasn't at all common to be able to get a really good curry. This place did all the classic stuff, like green curry, and I ate there as much as I could, all the way through university.

Later, I started cooking a lot of Thai food myself, after Katie and I went backpacking to Bangkok and Chiang Mai, and then on to Koh Samui and Koh Tao. Eating Thai food on the beach in Thailand was just one of the most amazing things. That's why I now insist on putting Thai curries on the LEON menu – they are a very powerful food memory for me.'

≡ TIP ≡

Chicken thighs have
more flavour, but use
chicken breast if you want a
neater-looking curry.

JUNGLE CURRY

SERVES 4
PREP TIME: 30 MINS • COOK TIME: 25 MINS
WF • GF • DF • NF • SoF

2–3 tablespoons **neutral cooking oil**

500g **aubergines**, cut into 2cm cubes

600ml hot **chicken stock**

8–10 **lime leaves**

800g skinless, boneless **chicken thighs**,
     cut into bite-sized pieces

150g **long green beans**

150g **baby corn**

leaves from 4 sprigs **Thai basil**

freshly squeezed **lime juice**, to taste

salt, to taste

Thai jasmine or **sticky rice**, to serve

FOR THE CURRY PASTE:

75g (2 medium) **shallots**, finely chopped

1–2 **hot red chillies** (deseeded or not,
     to taste)

1 stick of **lemongrass**, outer layer
     removed, finely chopped

3cm piece of **ginger**, peeled and
     finely grated

3 cloves of **garlic**, crushed

½ teaspoon **dried red chilli flakes**

2 teaspoons **fish sauce**

½ teaspoon **galangal paste**

1 tablespoon **very finely chopped
     coriander root** or **stalks** (optional)

½ teaspoon **ground coriander**

This Northern Thai curry is made without coconut (in the past, very few coconut palms grew in Northern Thailand). You can now buy jungle curry paste, if you don't have time to make it fresh.

Grind all the curry paste ingredients together until fairly smooth, using a pestle and mortar, spice grinder or small blender (or use about 3 tablespoons of a good-quality, ready-made jungle curry paste).

Heat 2 tablespoons of the oil in a large pan with a lid, set over a medium heat, add the spice paste and fry for 2–3 minutes, until really fragrant. Add the aubergines, plus the remaining oil if needed, and sauté for 4–5 minutes, stirring frequently so the paste doesn't stick and burn. Stir in the hot stock and lime leaves, scraping up any paste stuck to the bottom and sides of the pan, and bring up to a simmer. Add the chicken, partly cover with a lid and cook for 8 minutes, stirring once or twice.

Add the beans and baby corn, pushing them into the curry until submerged, then cover completely with the lid and simmer for 3 minutes. If the curry looks very thin (it should be soupy), remove the lid and increase the heat for a final 3–4 minutes. Remove from the heat and stir in most of the Thai basil, plus a good squeeze or two of lime juice. Taste for salt (or fish sauce or chilli), adding more as needed.

Divide the curry between 4 bowls. Garnish with the remaining Thai basil leaves and serve with rice on the side.

PORK VINDALOO

SERVES 4
PREP TIME: 20 MINS, PLUS 2–12 HOURS MARINATING • COOK TIME: 1 HOUR 10 MINS
WF • GF • DF • NF • SoF • SUITABLE FOR FREEZING

900g **pork shoulder**, fat trimmed, cut into large chunks
2 tablespoons **neutral cooking oil** or **ghee**
3 **onions**, finely sliced
1 teaspoon **mustard seeds**
1 teaspoon **tamarind paste** or **concentrate** (optional)
steamed rice, to serve

FOR THE MARINADE:
5 **cloves**
seeds from 6 **cardamom pods**
1 teaspoon **coriander seeds**
½ teaspoon **cumin seeds**
½ teaspoon **ground turmeric**
2 teaspoons **sweet paprika** (the reddest you can find)
¼ teaspoon **ground cinnamon**
¼ teaspoon **freshly ground black pepper**
½ teaspoon **hot chilli powder**
2 teaspoons **dried red chilli flakes** (or more for a really fiery vindaloo)
5 cloves of **garlic**, crushed
3cm piece of **ginger**, peeled and finely grated
3 tablespoons **red wine vinegar**
a generous pinch of **salt**

One of Rebecca's happiest holidays was travelling around south India with her now-husband Steve. They had no money and slept in beach huts, and it was wonderful. This hot-and-sour Goan-style vindaloo was created by Goan cooks and Portuguese colonialists centuries ago, when Goa was part of Portugal's vast empire. It comes from vinha d'alhos, a Portuguese meat stew made with vinegar.

To make the marinade, grind the whole spices to a powder in a pestle and mortar or spice grinder. Mix in the ground spices, chilli powder and chilli flakes, then mix in the garlic, ginger, vinegar and salt until well combined.

Use your hands to work the marinade into the pork, then cover and chill in the fridge for at least 2 hours or overnight.

When ready to cook, heat the oil in a large, heavy-based pan over a medium-high heat. Add the onions and cook for 10–12 minutes, stirring often, until the onions are golden. Add the mustard seeds and cook until they begin to crackle, 1–2 minutes. Add the marinated pork along with the marinade and cook for 5 minutes, stirring. Add 150ml hot water and stir well, scraping up anything that has stuck to the pan, and bring to the boil. Reduce the heat and gently simmer, uncovered, for 45 minutes, stirring every 10 minutes or so.

About 10 minutes before the end of cooking, stir through the tamarind concentrate, if using.

Taste for salt and chilli heat levels and adjust if necessary. If the sauce is still quite loose, increase the heat and allow it to reduce – a vindaloo should have a thick, rich gravy. Serve with steamed rice.

≡ TIP ≡

Don't worry about
the amount of vinegar
used here – although this is a
piquant curry, it doesn't taste
of vinegar.

BEEF MADRAS

2 tablespoons **neutral cooking oil** or **ghee**

2 **onions**, finely diced

1 medium **carrot**, very finely diced

3 cloves of **garlic**, crushed

4cm piece of **ginger**, peeled and finely grated

½–1 medium **green chilli** (deseeded or not, to taste)

1½ teaspoons **hot chilli powder**

1 heaped teaspoon **Madras curry powder**

1 teaspoon **paprika**

1½ teaspoons **ground cumin**

1 teaspoon **ground coriander**

1 teaspoon **ground turmeric**

550ml **hot water**, plus extra as needed

200g **passata**

800g **stewing beef**, cut into bite-sized pieces

2 teaspoons good-quality **apple cider vinegar**

salt and **freshly ground black pepper**

plain or **pilau rice**, to serve

Raita (see page 164), to serve

═ TIP ═

For that true curry house flavour, add a dollop of ghee to the finished curry and stir through, just before serving.

The Madras curry is a British curry house invention (not a bad thing) and has come to mean a very hot curry in a slow-cooked tomato-based sauce. Here is our favourite version.

Heat the oil or ghee in a large heavy-based pan with a lid, set over a medium-high heat. Add the onions and carrot and sauté until the onions are translucent and beginning to brown, 8–10 minutes. Add the garlic, ginger and chilli and cook for 2–3 minutes, until fragrant, but don't allow the mixture to catch and burn. Add the ground spices and cook, stirring, for 1 minute, then add 100ml of the water and mix to form a paste. Cook for about 5 minutes, until the water has evaporated, then add the passata and cook for 3–4 minutes, stirring.

Stir in the beef, remaining hot water and vinegar and season well with salt and black pepper, then cover with the lid and bring up to a gentle simmer. Reduce the heat to low and cook, covered, for 2–3 hours. Stir the curry occasionally so that nothing sticks to the bottom of the pan, and top up with water if necessary.

When the meat is meltingly tender and beginning to fall apart, remove the lid, turn the heat to medium and let the sauce reduce until it is very thick and coats each piece of meat. If you want a smooth sauce, use tongs to remove the meat and process the sauce to a purée with a stick blender, then return the meat to the pan.

Serve with plain or pilau rice and raita, or as part of a spread of curries with dhal and flatbreads.

CHIARA'S GRANDMOTHER'S GOAN-STYLE CHICKEN CAFREAL

SERVES 4

PREP TIME: 20 MINS, PLUS 12 HOURS MARINATING • COOK TIME: 45–55 MINS

WF • GF • DF • NF • SoF

4–8 (depending on size and hunger) skinless, bone-in **chicken thighs**

2 tablespoons **neutral cooking oil**

6cm stick of **cinnamon**

4 **green cardamom pods**

5 **black peppercorns**

2 **onions**, diced

½ teaspoon each **ground cumin**, **ground coriander** and **cumin seeds**

¼ teaspoon **ground turmeric**

1 tablespoon **desiccated coconut**

salt and **freshly ground black pepper**

coriander leaves and **rice** or **Indian flatbreads** (see pages 198–201), to serve

FOR THE MARINADE:

½ **onion**, diced

a handful of **fresh coriander**, finely chopped

3cm piece of **ginger**, peeled and grated

6 cloves of **garlic**, finely chopped

4 **green chillies** (deseeded or not, to taste), finely chopped

1 heaped teaspoon **coriander seeds**

1 tablespoon **apple cider vinegar**

LEON regular Chiara Pinto sent us this favourite family recipe. 'This has a green masala that coats the meat as a thick sauce – if you want more sauce you can add more water or even coconut milk. It was my grandmother's recipe and she added roasted coconut to thicken the sauce. We serve it with a soft bread called pao, but rice is good too.'

To make the marinade, grind the ingredients to a paste in a pestle and mortar or spice grinder. Make a couple of slashes in the thicker parts of the chicken thighs, then massage the paste into the meat. Cover and marinate in the fridge overnight.

When ready to cook, heat the oil in a large pan with a lid, over a medium heat. Add the cinnamon, cardamom pods and peppercorns and fry for 3 minutes, to flavour the oil. Remove from the pan, leaving the oil behind. Add the onions and cook for 6–8 minutes, stirring, until translucent. Add the ground spices and cumin seeds and fry for 1 minute. Stir in the chicken, its marinade and a splash of water, then cover with the lid and cook for 20 minutes, stirring regularly and adding 3–4 tablespoons of water every now and then, to stop it sticking. Meanwhile, in a small dry pan over a medium heat, toast the coconut until golden. Tip out of the pan immediately and grind to a fine powder in a pestle and mortar.

Add the coconut and some salt and pepper to the pan, re-cover and cook for a further 10–25 minutes, depending on the size of the chicken thighs, until done (pierce the meat to the bone – the juices should run clear).

To serve, sprinkle with a little fresh coriander, and eat with rice or flatbreads.

CARIBBEAN-STYLE BLACK BEAN CURRY

SERVES 2 AS A MAIN OR 4 AS A SIDE

PREP TIME: 20 MINS • COOK TIME: 25 MINS

WF • GF • DF • V • Ve • NF • SoF (check rotis)

1 tablespoon **neutral cooking oil**

1 **onion**, finely chopped

½ **red** or **orange pepper**, deseeded and diced

2 cloves of **garlic**, crushed

2cm piece of **ginger**, peeled and finely grated

10 sprigs of **fresh coriander**, stalks finely chopped, leaves reserved to garnish

1 teaspoon **mild** or **medium curry powder** (ideally Jamaican but Madras or similar will work)

¼ teaspoon **hot chilli powder** (optional)

400g can **cooked black beans in water**, undrained

1 sprig of **thyme**

1 **bay leaf**

2 tablespoons **coconut milk** or **coconut cream**

½ teaspoon **apple cider vinegar**

salt and **freshly ground black pepper**

1 **shallot**, finely sliced, to garnish

freshly squeezed **lime juice**, to serve

rice or **Rotis** (see page 200), to serve

Don't skip the toppings – the shallot and lime really make this curry sing.

Heat the oil in a saucepan set over a medium heat, add the onion and pepper and sauté for about 8 minutes, until softened and the onion is just beginning to brown. Add the garlic, ginger, coriander stalks, curry powder and chilli powder, if using. Cook, stirring, for 2–3 minutes, until fragrant. Add the beans along with the water from the can, the thyme and bay leaf and bring up to a simmer, then reduce the heat to low and gently simmer for 10 minutes, stirring every now and then (add a splash of water if the pan gets too dry).

Remove from the heat and add the coconut milk or coconut cream and the vinegar. Stir well, then taste for salt and pepper – add a touch more vinegar if you'd like more tang.

To serve, divide between bowls, then top each one with the reserved coriander leaves, sliced shallot and a little squeeze of lime juice. Eat with rice or roti, as a main, or alongside jerk chicken or tofu.

= TIP =

If you really like to make your tongue tingle, swap the green chilli for ¼ of a super-hot Scotch bonnet chilli, deseeded and finely diced (be sure to wash your hands or wear gloves).

CREAMY

SAG PANEER

SERVES 2 AS A MAIN OR 4 AS A SIDE
PREP TIME: 15 MINS • COOK TIME: 35 MINS
WF • GF • V • Ve (with substitutions, see tip) **• NF • SoF**

500g **spinach leaves**, large stems removed, leaves roughly chopped

50g **frozen fenugreek leaves**, defrosted (optional)

2 tablespoons **ghee** or **vegetable oil**

250g **paneer** (a firm Indian curd cheese), cut into rough 2cm cubes, patted dry with kitchen paper

1 **onion**, finely sliced

a pinch of **salt**

3 cloves of **garlic**, crushed

2cm piece of **ginger**, peeled and finely grated

1 teaspoon **garam masala**

½ teaspoon **turmeric**

a pinch of **cumin seeds**

a pinch of **freshly grated nutmeg**

a pinch of **dried red chilli flakes** (optional)

3–4 tablespoons **double cream**

a handful of **fresh coriander**, roughly chopped (optional)

freshly squeezed lemon juice, to taste

Once upon a time, Rebecca was a vegetarian. Her student house had a Wednesday ritual of watching **Sex and the City** *(the first series!) and getting a takeaway. This gloriously rich and creamy curry house favourite was always her order. In India, you might find it made without the cream, in which case a dollop of ghee, melted in at the end, is a good idea.*

Wash the spinach, then tip the wet leaves into a large pan with a lid, set over a medium heat. Steam along with the fenugreek leaves, if using, for 4–5 minutes, until the spinach has just wilted (work in batches if necessary). Drain and cool in a colander set over the sink.

Heat the ghee or oil in a large wide pan with a lid over a medium heat. When the ghee has melted, carefully add the paneer (it may splatter). Cook for just 1 minute or so on each side, then turn – you want it to be golden, but not dry. Use tongs to remove from the pan and set aside. Reduce the heat to low and add the onions to the pan, along with a pinch of salt. Cook for about 10 minutes, stirring, until soft and barely browned. Add the garlic, ginger, garam masala, turmeric and cumin seeds and cook for 3–4 minutes, stirring often.

Gently squeeze the excess water out of the cooled spinach (not too thoroughly, but it mustn't be soggy) and add it, along with the cooked paneer, to the pan. Add the nutmeg, chilli flakes, if using, and 3 tablespoons of the cream and cook briefly, stirring until well combined.

Remove from the heat and stir in the coriander leaves, if using, and squeeze over a little lemon juice. Taste and decide if you want to add more chilli flakes, cream, lemon or salt. Serve immediately.

=== TIP ===

Vegans can use
vegetable oil or vegan
ghee, leave out the cream
and substitute the paneer
for tofu, cooked in the
same way.

= TIP =

To make this more filling, add cooked chickpeas or cooked lentils when adding the beetroot. If you have any Sri Lankan roasted curry powder (see page 106), a pinch on top of the finished curry works wonders.

BEETROOT & COCONUT CURRY

SERVES 2 AS A MAIN OR 4 AS A SIDE
PREP TIME: 20 MINS • COOK TIME: 25 MINS
WF • GF • DF • V • Ve • NF • SoF

1 tablespoon **neutral cooking oil**

½ teaspoon **mustards seeds**

1 teaspoon **cumin seeds**

a pinch of **fenugreek seeds**

½ **onion**, finely sliced

2cm piece of **ginger**, peeled and finely grated

2 cloves of **garlic**, crushed

1 medium **green chilli**, finely chopped

½ teaspoon **ground coriander**

400g **beetroot**, peeled, quartered and sliced into ½cm pieces

100ml **water**

250ml **full-fat coconut milk**

1 tablespoon **desiccated coconut**

1 teaspoon finely chopped **red chilli**

1 tablespoon **finely chopped fresh coriander**

zest of ½ a **lime**

2 teaspoons freshly squeezed **lime juice**, or more to taste

salt and **freshly ground black pepper**

Earthy beetroot makes this curry almost sweet, but it is bolstered by chilli heat, sour lime and the coconut crunch of the topping.

Heat the oil in a large pan with a lid, set over a medium heat. Add the mustard seeds and, when they start to pop, add the cumin and fenugreek seeds and cook for 1 minute. Add the onion and cook for 5 minutes, then add the ginger, garlic and green chilli and cook, stirring, for 3–4 minutes. Add the ground coriander and cook for a further 1 minute.

Add the beetroot, water and 200ml of the coconut milk and bring up to a simmer. Partially cover with the lid, and simmer for about 20 minutes, or until the beetroot is just tender.

Meanwhile, make the topping. Set a small dry pan over a medium heat and add the desiccated coconut. Cook for 1–2 minutes, moving it around the pan just until it begins to brown, then immediately transfer it to a small bowl. Add the chopped chilli, coriander and lime zest, along with a pinch of salt and mix well.

When the beetroot is tender, add the remaining 50ml of coconut milk to the curry and just warm through a little. Remove from the heat and season to taste with lime juice and plenty of salt and freshly ground black pepper.

Serve each bowlful topped with a sprinkling of the toasted coconut mixture.

SHUMAIYA'S FAMILY CHICKEN KORMA

SERVES 8–10
PREP TIME: 20 MINS • COOK TIME: 1 HOUR
WF • GF • NF • SoF (check pilau/paratha)

4 tablespoons **ghee**

3 **onions**, finely sliced

1 teaspoon **pink Himalayan salt**, or
   ¾ teaspoon ordinary **salt**

6cm stick of **cinnamon**, roughly broken

½ teaspoon **cumin seeds**

3–5 **cloves**

3 **bay leaves**

4 **green cardamom pods**

½ teaspoon **black peppercorns**

1 teaspoon **ground white pepper**

3 cloves of **garlic**, minced

4cm piece of **ginger**, peeled and finely
   grated

3–5 **green chillies**, split lengthways,
   to taste

1.5kg **whole chicken**, cut into jointed
   portions on the bone, skin removed
   (or use the same weight of **thighs** and
   drumsticks)

10 **eggs**, at room temperature

a handful of **fresh coriander**, to garnish
   (optional)

Pilau (made without meat, see page 177)
   or **Paratha** (see page 205), to serve

When John gets takeaway, he orders curry from Nizam in Haywards Heath, and he doesn't even need to ask what his kids want: korma.

Our friend Shumi (or Shumaiya)'s family is from Bangladesh. 'A Bengali kulma (aka korma) is buttery and rich, and quite unlike what most of Britain knows as a korma. Its natural sweetness comes from slow-cooked onions and whole spices. Made for special occasions, this recipe has been passed down from generation to generation.'

Heat the ghee in a very large heavy-based pan with a lid, set over a medium-low heat. Add the onions, salt, spices, bay leaves, cardamom pods and black and white peppers. Cook until softened and slightly translucent, 10–15 minutes.

Add the garlic, ginger and chillies and cook until the onions are on the verge of becoming jammy and the oil separates from the mixture, about 10 minutes.

Increase the heat to medium and add the chicken, including the carcass. Stir, then cover with the lid and reduce the heat to low. Cook for 30 minutes, stirring occasionally until the chicken is thoroughly cooked and the juices have emulsified to a gravy. Don't let the juices dry up and, if needed, add around 100ml of water.

After 20 minutes cooking, bring a pan of water to the boil, add the eggs and cook for 7 minutes (don't hard-boil them). Drain and cool under running water, then peel and add to the chicken korma for the final 2 minutes of cooking to warm through.

Check seasoning, adding more as needed. If you used the chicken carcass, remove it now. Garnish with fresh coriander and serve with a plain (meatless) pilau or freshly cooked, crispy parathas.

≡ **TIP** ≡

This dish gets better
with age, so it is great
the next day.

≡ TIP ≡

Adding salt to the onions stops them from browning too quickly – a neat trick if you want soft, translucent onions in a dish.

NILGIRI CURRY

SERVES 4

PREP TIME: 25 MINS, PLUS 30 MINS–8 HOURS MARINATING • COOK TIME: 1 HOUR

Can be **WF • GF • DF • NF • SoF**

800g skinless, boneless **chicken thighs** or **breasts**, cut into bite-sized pieces

6 tablespoons **full-fat plain yoghurt** (or a rich **coconut** or **almond yoghurt**)

1 teaspoon **ground turmeric**

1 tablespoon **neutral cooking oil**

2 **onions**, finely chopped

seeds from 7 **green cardamom pods**

4 **cloves**

a large handful of **fresh coriander**, finely chopped, plus a little to garnish

6 sprigs of **mint**, finely chopped

2 medium **hot green chillies** (deseeded or not, to taste), finely chopped

about 250ml **cold water**, plus extra as needed

4cm piece of **ginger**, peeled and finely grated

3 cloves of **garlic**, crushed

a pinch of **fennel seeds**

½ teaspoon **ground cinnamon**

8 **curry leaves**

1 **bay leaf**

30g **unroasted cashew nuts**, chopped

4 tablespoons **full-fat coconut milk**

salt

rice or **Chapati** (see page 200), to serve

The Nilgiri mountains are in southern India. This fragrant green curry, made with heaps of coriander and mint, is originally from the local hill-station towns. At LEON, we believe in the power of fresh herbs, so this one is right up our street.

Combine the chicken in a bowl with the yoghurt, turmeric and ½ teaspoon of salt. Cover and marinate in the fridge for 30 minutes–8 hours.

Heat the oil in a large, wide, heavy-based pan over a medium heat. Add the onions and a pinch of salt and cook for about 8 minutes, stirring, until soft and translucent. Meanwhile, grind the cardamom seeds and cloves to a powder in a pestle and mortar.

Blitz the coriander, mint, chillies and cold water in a blender to a loose pesto texture.

Add the ginger, garlic, freshly ground spices, fennel seeds and ground cinnamon to the pan and cook for 3–4 minutes, stirring, until fragrant. Then, add the herb mixture to the pan, along with the curry leaves, bay leaf, the chicken and all of its marinade, and bring up to a simmer.

Grind the cashew nuts in the pestle and mortar, as finely as you can, then add them to the pan, cover and simmer for 30 minutes. Give it a stir halfway through and add a little water if it is drying out.

At the end of cooking, uncover the pan. If there is a lot of liquid (the herbs will release a little during cooking), increase the heat and let it reduce for 3–5 minutes. Add the coconut milk, then taste and add salt, if needed.

Serve sprinkled with the extra coriander, with rice or chapati alongside.

LAMB PASANDA

SERVES 4

PREP TIME: 20 MINS, PLUS 30 MINS–8 HOURS MARINATING • COOK TIME: 1 HOUR

WF • GF • SoF • SUITABLE FOR FREEZING

700g **lamb leg** (steaks or large pieces), cut into thin slices

7 tablespoons **full-fat plain yoghurt**

6 tablespoons **single cream**

5 tablespoons **ground almonds**

4cm piece of **ginger**, peeled and finely grated

3 cloves of **garlic**, crushed

1 teaspoon **ground coriander**

1 teaspoon **ground turmeric**

1 teaspoon **paprika**

¼–½ teaspoon **chilli powder**, to taste

1 teaspoon **ground cumin**

1 tablespoon **neutral cooking oil**

1 large **onion**, finely sliced

½–1 **green chilli** (deseeded or not, to taste), finely chopped

½ teaspoon **cumin seeds**

a pinch of **fenugreek seeds** (optional)

6 **green cardamom pods**

¼ teaspoon **ground cinnamon**

a pinch of **freshly ground nutmeg**

4 **cloves**

salt

450ml **hot water**

basmati rice, to serve

*A creamy and mild curry that you will always, **always**, find on the menu in British curry houses.*

Arrange the lamb slices in a single layer on a chopping board, cover with clingfilm and bash with a rolling pin (or meat mallet) until thin. In a large bowl, mix together 6 tablespoons of the yoghurt with the cream, ground almonds, ginger, garlic and ground spices. Cover and marinate in the fridge for 30 minutes, or overnight.

When ready to cook, heat the oil in a large deep saucepan with a lid over a medium-low heat. Add the onion and gently cook for 10–12 minutes, until browned. Add the green chilli, cumin seeds, fenugreek seeds, if using, cardamom pods, cinnamon, nutmeg and cloves, along with a pinch of salt. Cook for about 2 minutes, stirring, until the spices are fragrant.

Add the lamb and all the marinade and cook for 1–2 minutes, stirring, then reduce the heat and add the hot water. Cover and bring up to a gentle simmer and cook for 45 minutes, stirring now and then. Remove the lid about halfway through, so that the liquid can reduce.

When the oil rises to the top of the curry, it is ready. Taste a piece of the lamb – it should be very tender. If necessary, increase the heat to reduce the gravy; the curry should be saucy, but not wet. Remove from the heat and stir through the remaining yoghurt.

Serve immediately, with rice.

≡ TIP ≡

Save time by batch-cooking double the quantity of meatballs and then freezing them. If you have any Thai basil (not always easy to find), add a handful of leaves before serving.

CHICKEN MEATBALL COCONUT CURRY

SERVES 4
PREP TIME: 20 MINS • COOK TIME: 33 MINS
WF • GF • DF • NF • SoF

1 tablespoon **neutral cooking oil**

700g skinless, boneless **chicken thighs** (or **minced chicken** or **turkey**)

2 tablespoons good-quality **Thai red curry paste** (or use the recipe on page 43)

4 **spring onions**, finely chopped

600ml **full-fat coconut milk**

1 clove of **garlic**, crushed

2 teaspoons **fish sauce** (or a good pinch of **salt**)

6 **lime leaves**, torn

1 stick of **lemongrass**, whole, bashed flat with a rolling pin

½–1 teaspoon **dried red chilli flakes**, to taste

½ teaspoon **ground coriander**

½ teaspoon **ground cumin**

½ teaspoon **ground turmeric**

100g **long green beans**, trimmed

150g **asparagus**, trimmed and split lengthways

100g **baby corn**, split lengthways

1 head **pak choi**, leaves split lengthways, cut into bite-sized pieces

steamed rice or **Thai noodles**, to serve

This is incredibly quick and easy to prepare, but looks and tastes amazing. We were inspired to create this recipe because LEON's Sicilian Meatballs are so popular.

Heat the oven to 200°C/400°F/gas mark 6 and grease a large roasting pan with the oil.

Place the chicken, red curry paste, three-quarters of the spring onions and a pinch of salt into a food processor and blitz to mince the chicken (if using mince, just mix everything together). Shape the mince into 20 meatballs, about the size of ping-pong balls. Place in the roasting pan and bake for 10 minutes. Remove from the oven and use tongs to turn each one, then bake for a further 10 minutes.

Meanwhile, in a large bowl, mix together the coconut milk, garlic, fish sauce or salt, remaining spring onions, lime leaves, lemongrass, chilli flakes and ground spices.

Remove the roasting pan from the oven and add the vegetables. Pour over the coconut mixture, then toss everything together. Arrange the meatballs and vegetables roughly in a single layer in the dish, making sure the lime leaves and pak choi leaves are submerged.

Bake for 5 minutes, then remove to shake everything around and turn the meatballs one last time. Return to the oven for a final 8 minutes.

Taste the broth for seasoning. Serve with steamed rice or Thai noodles.

ERICA'S LENTIL MASALA

SERVES 4

PREP TIME: 20 MINS • COOK TIME: 50 MINS

WF • GF • DF • V • Ve • NF • SoF (check stock)

150g **uncooked lentils**

1 tablespoon **neutral cooking oil**

½ teaspoon each **cumin** and **mustard seeds**

1 small **onion**, half finely sliced, half grated

2 cloves of **garlic**, crushed

1 teaspoon **peeled and finely grated ginger**

½ **green chilli**, deseeded and finely diced

1 small **carrot**, very finely diced

½ **celery stick**, finely diced

1 teaspoon **ground cumin**

1 teaspoon **ground coriander**

1½ teaspoons **sweet smoked paprika**

2 heaped teaspoons **medium curry powder**

1 tablespoon **apple cider vinegar**

2 teaspoons **tomato purée**

100ml **passata**

200ml **full-fat coconut milk**

150ml good-quality **vegetable** or **vegan stock**

½ **butternut squash**, peeled, cut into 1cm pieces

75g **kale** or **spring greens**, stems and ribs removed, finely shredded

salt and **freshly ground black pepper**

freshly squeezed lemon juice, to serve

brown or **white rice**, to serve

Erica Molyneaux is LEON's head of food (best job title ever?) and created this autumnal vegan recipe for the LEON menu last year. You can use any kind of lentils, but we love chana dal/split yellow gram, as they hold their shape.

Place the uncooked lentils in a saucepan and cover with 5cm depth of cold water. Bring to the boil, then reduce the heat and simmer until tender but not turning to mush (how long depends on which lentil you choose – red lentils take around 20 minutes; chana dal can take as long as 50 minutes).

Meanwhile, heat the oil in a large, deep pan with a lid over a medium heat. When hot, add the cumin and mustard seeds. As soon as the mustard seeds start to pop, add the sliced and grated onion, garlic, ginger, chilli, carrot and celery. Cook for 6 minutes, stirring often, until the sliced onion is translucent. Add all the spices and cook for 1 minute, stirring, until fragrant. Mix in 100ml water, then gently simmer for about 5 minutes, stirring now and then. When the water has evaporated, the mixture seems thick and glossy, and oil is rising to the top, add the vinegar and tomato purée. Cook for 3–4 minutes, then add the passata, coconut milk, stock and butternut squash. Bring up to a simmer, cover and cook for 25 minutes, until the squash is done – it should hold its shape, so don't let it overcook.

Taste the curry and add salt and pepper, as needed. For the last 3–4 minutes of cooking, stir through the kale and the cooked lentils.

Serve over rice, with a squeeze of lemon to finish.

=≡ TIP ≡=

Switch the squash
for pumpkin or sweet
potato, and use spinach or
any other wilt-able greens,
instead of kale.

== TIP ==

Using bone-in chicken gives more flavour, but for speed you can use boneless (use 600g and halve the cooking time). In Thailand, this is served topped with crunchy deep-fried noodles. To make your own: blanch and pat dry an extra 100g egg noodles, then briefly fry in 2cm hot oil, until crisp.

KHAO SOI GAI

SERVES 4

PREP TIME: 20 MINS • COOK TIME: 50 MINS

DF • NF • SoF (check stock)

2 teaspoons **coriander seeds**

seeds from 4 **green cardamom pods**

2 tablespoons **finely grated turmeric root** (optional)

4cm piece of **ginger**, peeled and grated

1 tablespoon **very finely chopped coriander stalks**

4 tablespoons **Thai red curry paste**

1 tablespoon **neutral cooking oil**

600ml **full-fat coconut milk**

400ml hot **chicken stock**

8 **lime leaves**, roughly torn

1 teaspoon **fish sauce**, or more to taste

900g bone-in **chicken thighs** and **drumsticks** (ideally 8 small pieces), skin on or off

200g **Asian leafy greens**, sliced into 3cm pieces (we use choy sum)

240g **dried medium egg noodles**

salt

TO SERVE:

a handful of **fresh coriander**

crispy onions (bought or homemade, see page 179)

a drizzle of **spicy chilli oil** (optional)

lime wedges

This curried noodle soup is from Chiang Mai in Northern Thailand, but is related to dishes found in neighbouring Burma. Find turmeric root next to the fresh ginger in large supermarkets.

Grind the dry spices to a powder in a pestle and mortar. Add the turmeric, ginger and coriander stalks and pound to a paste. Add the red curry paste and mix well.

Heat the oil in a very large, deep, heavy-based pan, over a medium heat. When hot, add the spice paste and cook, stirring, for 4–5 minutes, until really fragrant. Reduce the heat to low, add half the coconut milk and bring up to a simmer, then add the rest along with the stock, lime leaves and fish sauce. Bring up to a simmer again. Make a few deep slashes down to the bone in the chicken, then submerge in the broth and cook, covered, for 30 minutes. Halfway through, turn each piece of chicken over to ensure they cook all the way through.

Meanwhile, bring a large pan of salted water to the boil.

Check the chicken is done by piercing a thick piece; if the juices run clear it is cooked (if not, cook for a further 5–10 minutes). Stir the greens into the pan, cover and cook for 3 minutes.

Blanch the noodles in the boiling water for 2–3 minutes, until al dente. Drain and refresh under a little running cold water so they don't become soggy, and divide among 4 wide shallow bowls.

Taste the curry and add a little more fish sauce if needed. Place 1 or 2 pieces of chicken into each bowl on top of the noodles, then ladle the curry and greens over. Finish with coriander, some crispy onions, a drizzle of chilli oil and lime wedges.

CHICKEN CHETTINAD

SERVES 4

PREP TIME: 10 MINS, PLUS 1 HOUR MARINATING • COOK TIME: 1 HOUR

WF • GF • SoF (check flatbreads) • **SUITABLE FOR FREEZING**

600g skinless, boneless **chicken thighs** or **breasts**, cut into large chunks

5 tablespoons **full-fat plain yoghurt**

1½ teaspoons **hot chilli powder** (to taste)

1 teaspoon **sweet paprika**

½ teaspoon **ground turmeric**

1 tablespoon **neutral cooking oil**

2 **onions**, finely sliced

10 **curry leaves**

3cm piece of **ginger**, peeled and finely grated

3 cloves of **garlic**, crushed

200g **chopped tomatoes** (fresh or canned)

salt and **freshly ground black pepper**

a handful of **fresh coriander**, to garnish

rice or **Indian flatbreads** (see pages 198–201 and 205–6), to serve

FOR THE SPICE BLEND:

1 teaspoon each **cumin** and **coriander seeds**

½ teaspoon **fennel seeds**

4 **cloves**

a pinch of **ground cinnamon**

2 tablespoons chopped **cashew nuts**

seeds from 3 **green cardamom pods**

4 tablespoons **desiccated coconut**

This nifty recipe is from Tamil Nadu in India. Using cashews and desiccated coconut in the sauce makes it rich and thick, without needing buckets of cream.

Place the chicken in a bowl with the yoghurt, chilli powder, paprika and turmeric. Mix well, then cover and place in the fridge for at least 1 hour, or as long as overnight.

When ready to cook, set a large frying pan over a medium heat. Add all the spice blend ingredients and toast, stirring frequently, for 3–4 minutes, until the spices smell wonderful and the coconut is golden. Tip everything into a spice grinder or pestle and mortar and grind to a fine powder. Add 2 tablespoons water and mix to form a paste.

Heat the oil in a large, deep pan with a lid over a medium heat. When hot, add the onions and cook, stirring often, until they are beginning to turn golden brown. Add the curry leaves, ginger and garlic and sizzle for about 5 minutes, stirring now and then and taking care not to let it burn, then add the tomatoes, and cook, stirring again, for 3–4 minutes. Scrape the chicken and all of its marinade into the pan, then tip in the spice paste and mix. Cook for 2 minutes, then add just enough water to make everything saucy, about 100–150ml. Add a good pinch of salt and a generous dusting of black pepper, stir, then cover and cook for about 25 minutes, until the chicken is cooked through and tender. If it seems at all wet, uncover the pan for the last 5 minutes or so of the cooking time.

Garnish with a little fresh coriander and serve with rice or Indian flatbreads.

≡ TIP ≡

Vegetarians and vegans
can swap the meat for potatoes,
cauliflower and beans, or any root
vegetables, and the yoghurt for coconut
or almond yoghurt. The sauce is robust,
so if you want to use bone-in meat or
something needing longer cooking,
such as lamb, just add more water
and let simmer.

SRI LANKAN-STYLE COCONUT DHAL

SERVES 2–3 AS A MAIN OR 4–6 AS A SIDE WITH OTHER DISHES
PREP TIME: 15 MINS • COOK TIME: 28 MINS
WF • GF • DF • V • Ve • NF • SoF • SUITABLE FOR FREEZING

300g **split red lentils**

500ml **cold water**, or more as needed

½ teaspoon **ground turmeric**

4 tablespoons **neutral cooking oil**

1 teaspoon **mustard seeds**

½ teaspoon **cumin seeds**

a generous pinch of **fenugreek seeds**

6 **curry leaves**

1 small **onion**, finely sliced

1 medium **green chilli**, finely chopped

2 cloves of **garlic**, crushed

6 tablespoons **coconut cream**

salt and **freshly ground black pepper**

This is something you'll often find – albeit made in lots of different ways – in a Sri Lankan home-cooked meal. This is our version.

Rinse the red lentils a couple of times in cold water and drain. Place the lentils in a large pan with a lid, cover with the cold water, add the turmeric and bring up to a simmer. Use a slotted spoon to skim off any scum that rises to the surface. Reduce the heat to low and cook for 15–20 minutes, stirring every now and then and topping up with water if necessary, until the lentils are tender and just beginning to collapse.

Meanwhile, heat the oil in a small frying pan set over a medium heat. Add the mustard seeds and, when they start to pop, add the cumin seeds, fenugreek seeds and curry leaves. Let the seeds toast for 1 minute or so, then add the onion. Cook for 8–10 minutes, stirring very frequently, until the onion begins to brown. Add the chilli, the garlic and a pinch of salt (to help the onions release their juices and stop the garlic burning), and cook for 3 minutes. Remove from the heat.

Spoon the coconut cream into the cooked lentils and cook for 3 minutes, stirring. Remove from the heat and tip the contents of the onion pan into the lentil dhal. Mix well, then taste for salt and season generously.

Serve immediately, with rice, breads and something yoghurt-y, or as part of a spread of curries.

= TIP =

If you leave out the chillies and cut back on the salt, this is an excellent meal for small kids. Rebecca freezes portions of it in reusable cupcake cases – perfect portions for toddlers.

LEMONGRASS COCONUT AUBERGINE CURRY

SERVES 4
PREP TIME: 15 MINS • COOK TIME: 30 MINS
WF • GF • DF • V • Ve • SoF

4 medium **aubergines**, stem ends trimmed, halved crossways, then cut into 2cm wedges

3 tablespoons **neutral cooking oil**

600ml **full-fat coconut milk**

2 sticks of **lemongrass**, bashed with a rolling pin until almost flat

4 **spring onions**, roughly chopped

2 cloves of **garlic**, crushed

8 **lime leaves**, roughly torn

1 teaspoon **ground turmeric**

1 teaspoon **ground cumin**

a generous pinch of **dried red chilli flakes** (optional)

50g **roasted unsalted peanuts**, chopped

finely grated zest of ½ **lime** (unwaxed)

salt

This simple curry packs way more punch than its quick-and-easy prep suggests.

Heat the oven to 200°C/400°F/gas mark 6.

Put the wedges of aubergine and the oil into a roasting pan and use your hands to toss it all together, making sure each piece is lightly coated in the oil. Roast for 20 minutes, turning the wedges halfway through.

Meanwhile, in a large bowl, combine the coconut milk, smashed lemongrass, spring onions, garlic, lime leaves, turmeric, cumin, chilli flakes, if using, and a good pinch of salt. Mix well.

Remove the aubergine pan from the oven and pour the coconut mixture over the aubergine wedges, turning each one to ensure they are all coated in the coconut curry. Return to the oven for a further 10 minutes.

Tip the peanuts onto a baking tray, and pop them in the oven for the last 7 minutes of the curry's cooking time.

Remove both pan and tray from the oven and set the aubergine curry aside, while you tip the nuts into a pestle and mortar and lightly pummel. Add the lime zest and a small pinch of salt.

Remove and discard the lime leaves and lemongrass from the aubergine curry, then serve the aubergine curry sprinkled with the peanut and lime zest topping.

SOUTH INDIAN-STYLE FISH CURRY

SERVES 4
PREP TIME: 15 MINS • COOK TIME: 35 MINS
WF • GF • DF • NF • SoF (check flatbreads)

1 tablespoon **neutral cooking oil**

1 teaspoon **mustard seeds**

6 **curry leaves**

1 **onion**, finely sliced

¼ teaspoon **cumin seeds**

4 **cloves**

4 **green cardamom pods**

2 cloves of **garlic**

3cm piece of **ginger**, peeled and grated

2 **green chillies**, deseeded and finely chopped

100g (about 1 large) **tomato**, deseeded and finely chopped

1 teaspoon **ground turmeric**

¼–½ teaspoon **hot chilli powder**

400ml **full-fat coconut milk**

400g **firm white fish** (**salmon** or **trout**, or a mixture), cut into large chunks

300g **courgette**, halved and sliced into ½cm strips

12–16 large **raw prawns**, depending on size

a pinch of **salt** and **freshly ground black pepper**

freshly squeezed lemon or **lime juice**, to taste

rice or **Indian flatbreads** (pages 198–201 and 205–6), to serve

This is based on a famous dish called meen moilee. To make it vegan, just add more vegetables along with the courgette – green beans, peas, snap peas, sliced peppers, cooked squash or sweet potato. Shellfish also work brilliantly – just cook for 3–4 minutes in the broth with the lid on.

Heat the oil in a large pan with a lid, set over a medium heat. When hot, add the mustard seeds and curry leaves and, when the seeds start to pop, add the onion, salt, cumin seeds, cloves and cardamom pods. Cook for 6–8 minutes, stirring, until the onions are soft but not brown. Add the garlic, ginger, chillies, tomato, turmeric and chilli powder and cook for a further 5–8 minutes, until the tomato has broken down and the mixture is fragrant, with a glossy, oily sheen.

Reduce the heat to low, add about one-quarter of the coconut milk and bring up to the boil, then add the rest of the coconut milk. Increase the heat to medium and bring to a simmer. Season with some black pepper, then taste and add more chilli powder if you'd like more heat.

Add the fish and courgettes to the pan, gently pressing them into the broth. Cover with a lid and cook for 4 minutes, then remove the lid and add the prawns, pressing them into the broth, but being careful not to break up the fish too much. Cover again and cook for a final 2 minutes. When you remove the lid, the fish should be cooked through and the prawns pink throughout.

Remove from the heat. Taste and add a squeeze of lemon or lime juice, if needed, then serve immediately with rice or Indian flatbreads.

WEST AFRICAN-STYLE PEANUT CURRY

SERVES 4

PREP TIME: 20 MINS • COOK TIME: 55 MINS

WF • GF • DF • V • Ve • SoF

1 tablespoon **neutral cooking oil**

2 **onions**, finely diced

2 cloves of **garlic**, crushed

2cm piece of **ginger**, peeled and grated

½ **red pepper**, deseeded and finely diced

2 teaspoons **tomato purée**

½ teaspoon **ground coriander**

½ teaspoon **ground cumin**

½ teaspoon **ground turmeric**

½–1 teaspoon **cayenne pepper**

400g **canned chopped tomatoes**, undrained

400ml **hot water**

50g **smooth peanut butter** (unsweetened)

600g (2 medium) **sweet potatoes**, peeled and diced

400g **canned cooked chickpeas**, drained

150g **kale**, or any sweet, soft-leaved **green cabbage**, stems and ribs removed, finely shredded

50g **okra**, trimmed and cut into 1cm rounds (optional)

salt and freshly ground **black pepper**

1 **red chilli**, deseeded and finely sliced, to serve

a handful of **toasted unsalted peanuts**, chopped, to serve

There are so many of our favourite LEON ingredients in this, that it makes us hum tunes from The Sound of Music: *kale, sweet potato, chickpeas, chillies and earthy, warming spices.*

Heat the oil in a large heavy-based pan over a medium heat. Add the onion and sauté gently for about 8 minutes, until soft. Add the garlic, ginger and red pepper and cook for 3–4 minutes, until fragrant. Add the tomato purée and all the ground spices (use only ½ teaspoon cayenne pepper to begin with) and cook for 2 minutes, stirring all the time, until fragrant.

Add the tomatoes and their juice, the water (just fill the tomato can), peanut butter and sweet potatoes. Stir well, then bring up to a simmer. Partly cover with a lid, reduce the heat and gently cook until the sweet potatoes are tender, about 20–25 minutes.

Add the drained chickpeas to the pan and simmer for another 5–10 minutes, then add the kale and okra, if using. Stir well, then simmer for a further 5 minutes, just until the kale is done. Remove from the heat and taste for salt and pepper. You can even add a pinch more cayenne, if you like.

Serve with the fresh red chilli slices and chopped peanuts, sprinkled on top.

TIP

If you only have crunchy peanut butter, no worries – you will just end up with a nuttier texture.

SPEEDY

SKINNY PARCEL-BAKED SALMON & COURGETTE CURRY

SERVES 2
PREP TIME: 15 MINS • COOK TIME: 25 MINS
WF • GF • DF • NF • SoF

1 teaspoon **fennel seeds**

4 **green cardamom pods**

1 tablespoon **neutral cooking oil**

1 teaspoon peeled and finely grated **ginger**

1 clove of **garlic**, crushed

2 tablespoons (about 1) finely grated **shallot**

1 teaspoon **ground coriander**

½ teaspoon **ground cumin**

½ teaspoon **ground turmeric**

1 teaspoon **tamarind paste** or
   concentrate (optional)

1 tablespoon **freshly squeezed lime juice**

3 tablespoons **full-fat coconut milk**

a pinch of **sugar**

2 skinless **salmon fillets** (or any fish fillets)

300g **courgette**, cut into ½cm slices on
   an angle

salt and **freshly ground black pepper**

steamed **wild and basmati rice**, to serve

lemon wedges, to serve

≡ TIP ≡

Switch the courgettes for any other crisp green veg – beans, asparagus or a mixture. Make it more of a one-pot dish by adding sliced cooked new potatoes to the parcel.

This is a super-light and low-fat curry, which is also very simple to make.

Place the fennel seeds and cardamom pods in a pestle and mortar (or use a rolling pin) and lightly bash, just to bruise and release their flavour. Tip into a large bowl with the oil, ginger, garlic, shallot, ground coriander, cumin, turmeric and tamarind concentrate, if using. Stir in the lime juice, coconut milk, sugar, a good pinch of salt and some freshly ground black pepper. Mix to form a paste. Add the salmon fillets and courgette slices to the bowl, mix well and use your hands to rub the paste into each piece.

Heat the oven to 180°C/350°F/gas mark 4.

Tear off a long sheet of baking paper or foil and lay it on top of a baking sheet so that one of the shorter sides is closest to you. Arrange the courgette slices in a rough layer in the centre of the paper or foil, about 2 slices thick. Top with the salmon, then scrape any remaining paste from the bowl and dot it on top. Bring the long sides of the paper or foil together over the fish and fold down, then fold the short ends together several times, enclosing the fish tightly and completely so that the steam cannot escape.

Bake for 25 minutes. When you unwrap the parcel, the courgettes should be just tender and the fish should be cooked through.

Serve with wild and basmati rice and lemon wedges.

CORNERSHOP CURRY

1 tablespoon **neutral cooking oil**

2 **onions**, finely diced

5 tablespoons **Indian-style curry paste from a jar** (we like fiery Madras)

300g **canned chopped tomatoes**, undrained

400g **canned cooked green beans**, drained

3 x 125g **canned mackerel fillets** (ideally in oil), drained

ready-made flatbreads or **microwave rice**, to serve

It's cold. It's ages until payday. You're knackered… So make this! It will warm you up and soothe your soul. And, we promise, it's all made with things you can find in the shop at the end of the road. (Rebecca invented this curry when in need of something better than beans on toast but almost as quick, on a day filled with deadlines. She has also been known to fry spice paste from a jar and then mix it with a tin of lentil soup – cheat's dhal!)

Heat the oil in a large heavy-based pan set over a medium heat. Add the onions and sauté gently for about 8 minutes, until soft. Add the curry paste and fry, stirring, for about 3 minutes. Add 50ml of the water and mix well, then simmer for a few minutes until most of the water has evaporated and the paste has a glossy, oily sheen.

Add the tomatoes, spooning them out of the can and leaving most of the juice behind. Reduce the heat to low, stir well and break up any lumps with the back of the spoon, then simmer for 8–10 minutes, or until the tomatoes have melted into the sauce.

Add the beans and the mackerel, plus another 50–100ml water, if the curry looks at all dry. Stir gently, being careful not to break up the fish too much, then cover with a lid. Increase the heat to medium, bring to a simmer and cook for 3–4 minutes, until everything is heated through.

Serve with ready-made flatbreads (or even pitta breads), or microwaved rice.

≡ TIP ≡

Mix and match with other cans from your local shop – use sardines, or go veggie and use cooked lentils, chickpeas or cannellini beans; experiment with other canned veg – peas, potatoes or carrots.

BAKED MACKEREL CURRY

SERVES 4

PREP TIME: 20 MINS • COOK TIME: 40 MINS

WF • GF • DF • NF • SoF

700g **new** or **baby potatoes**, halved

½ head **fennel**, finely sliced

1 large **onion**, finely sliced

500g **cherry tomatoes**, halved

1½ tablespoons **neutral cooking oil**

4 small whole **mackerel**, cleaned and gutted

salt, to taste

FOR THE SPICE PASTE:

2 teaspoons **ground turmeric**

4cm piece of **ginger**, peeled and grated

3 cloves of **garlic**, crushed

1 tablespoon **mustard seeds**

1 tablespoon **fennel seeds**

¼ teaspoon **salt**

2 teaspoons **coriander seeds**

2 teaspoons **cumin seeds**

a generous grinding of **black pepper**

1 **red chilli** (deseeded or not, to taste),
    finely chopped

FOR THE GREENS:

350g **chard** or **spinach**, stems removed

2 teaspoons **neutral cooking oil**

1 teaspoon **black mustard seeds**

1 clove of **garlic**, crushed

a pinch of **salt**

We love a baked curry – they are so easy. We also love heart-healthy mackerel, so we invented this.

Heat the oven to 200°C/400°F/gas mark 6.

Bring a large saucepan of salted water to the boil, then parboil the potatoes for 9 minutes. Drain.

Tip the potatoes into a large roasting pan (or two smaller ones) and add the fennel, onion, cherry tomatoes and 1 tablespoon of the oil. Toss until everything is coated in the oil, then roast in the oven for 15 minutes.

Meanwhile, grind the spice paste ingredients to a paste in a pestle and mortar.

Remove the pan from the oven, add two-thirds of the spice paste to the vegetables and toss together thoroughly. Rub the mackerel, inside and out, with the remaining third of the spice paste, drizzle with the remaining ½ tablespoon of oil and rest the fish on top of the vegetables. Sprinkle with a pinch of salt and return to the oven for a further 10 minutes.

Remove the pan from the oven, add about 50ml water and return to the oven for a final 5 minutes.

Meanwhile, make the greens. Wash the chard or spinach and drain in a colander, but do not dry. Heat the oil in a wide pan over a medium heat. When hot, add the mustard seeds and, as soon as they begin to pop, add the garlic and salt and cook for 1 minute, stirring. Add the freshly washed greens and cook for 3–4 minutes, stirring, until wilted. Serve the fish with the pan-baked curry, with the greens on the side.

CHANA MASALA

SERVES 2 AS A MAIN OR 4 AS A SIDE
PREP TIME: 15 MINS • COOK TIME: 35 MINS
WF • GF • DF • V • VE • NF • SoF

1 tablespoon **neutral cooking oil**

1 **onion**, finely sliced

2 teaspoons **mustard seeds**

1½ teaspoons **cumin seeds**

3cm piece of **ginger,** peeled and grated

2 cloves of **garlic**, crushed

10 **curry leaves**

1 teaspoon **ground coriander**

1 teaspoon **garam masala**

1 tablespoon **finely chopped green chilli**
(or more for a hotter curry)

200g **chopped tomatoes** (fresh and
skinned, or canned, or use passata)

400g **canned chickpeas**, undrained
(canned kala chana, brown chickpeas,
are ideal)

salt, to taste

squeeze of **lemon juice**, to serve

a generous handful of **fresh coriander**, to
garnish (optional)

═ TIP ═

If you happen to have some sour green
mango powder (amchoor/amchur)
lying around, then a pinch works
brilliantly here, as does a spoonful of
tamarind concentrate or paste.

Chickpeas have always been our friends at LEON. We have had them on the menu, in the form of hummus, every day since we opened our first LEON on Carnaby Street in 2004. This is easy, vegan and scrumptious.

Heat the oil in a large saucepan with a lid over a medium heat. When hot, add the onion and cook for about 8 minutes, stirring often, until beginning to brown. Add the mustard and cumin seeds and cook for a minute or so, until the mustard seeds begin to pop, then add the ginger, garlic, curry leaves, ground coriander, garam masala and chilli. Cook for 5 minutes, stirring, so that the garlic and ginger don't stick and burn.

Finally, add the chopped tomatoes and the chickpeas, along with the water from the can. Stir well to combine, then reduce the heat to low, cover with a lid and simmer gently for about 15 minutes. Check every now and then to make sure the pan isn't drying out, and add a splash of water if needed.

Taste and decide if you want to add any salt (some brands of chickpea are rather salty). Remove from the heat and, just before serving, add a squeeze of lemon juice and some fresh coriander leaves.

TOFU PHAD PHRIK KHING

SERVES 4

PREP TIME: 20 MINS • COOK TIME: 20 MINS

WF • GF • DF • V • VE • NF • SoF

500g **extra-firm tofu**, cut into 2 x 2cm
squares, about 1cm thick

2–4 tablespoons **neutral cooking oil**

3 tablespoons good-quality **Thai red
curry paste** (choose a vegan brand if
necessary, or use the recipe on page 43
omitting the fish sauce)

200g **long green beans**, cut into
3cm pieces

200g **Asian greens** (we like choy sum),
sliced into 3cm strips

75g **broccoli**, cut into bite-sized pieces

4 **lime leaves**, stems removed, leaves
sliced into very thin 1–2mm strips

2–3 tablespoons **water**

freshly squeezed lime juice

salt

steamed jasmine rice, to serve

*This dry Thai curry is usually made just with long green beans, but
we like to add extra greenery for goodness and flavour. If you like your
curries hot, taste the curry paste first – you may want to add extra fresh
or dried red chillies.*

Line a large plate or chopping board with 2 sheets of kitchen paper and arrange
the tofu in a single layer on top. Cover with more kitchen paper and use your hands
or another board to gently press out as much liquid as you can – this will result in
crisper tofu when cooked.

Heat 2 tablespoons of the oil in a large frying pan or wok set over a medium heat.
Working in batches if necessary and adding more oil as needed, fry the tofu until
golden on both sides, about 4 minutes per side. Don't try to move the tofu too
soon – it will stick at first and then gradually release from the pan as it cooks. Set
the cooked tofu aside and keep warm.

If the pan looks dry, add another tablespoon of oil, then add the curry paste and
cook, stirring, for 1 minute. Add the beans, greens, broccoli and lime leaves, plus
1 tablespoon of water and sauté for 3 minutes, moving everything around constantly
and adding more of the water if the pan is very dry.

Remove from the heat, gently stir in the hot tofu and coat in the sauce. Squeeze over
a little lime juice, then taste and add salt as needed (how much, if any, will depend on
the type of curry paste you used). Serve alongside a mound of jasmine rice.

≡ TIP ≡

Non-vegans may like to splash
in a little fish sauce, which is a
traditional Thai ingredient.

QUICKEST CURRY EVER

SERVES 2 AS A MAIN OR 4 AS A SIDE
PREP TIME: 15 MINS • COOK TIME: 13–14 MINS
WF • GF • DF • V • VE • NF • SoF

2 tablespoons **neutral cooking oil**

1 small **onion**, finely sliced

1 teaspoon **paprika**

½ teaspoon **chilli powder**

¼ teaspoon **ground turmeric**

½ teaspoon **ground cumin**

¼ teaspoon **ground coriander**

2 teaspoons **tomato purée**

1 medium **tomato**, deseeded, cored and finely diced

3cm piece of **ginger**, peeled and finely grated

2 cloves of **garlic**, crushed

125g **carrot**, peeled and cut into thin slivers

1 **sweet pepper**, deseeded and finely sliced

200g **cauliflower**, broken into very small florets

125g **long green beans**, finely sliced on an angle

1 **hot green chilli**, finely chopped

3 tablespoons **water**

salt and **freshly ground black pepper**

Naan (see page 198), to serve

a handful of **fresh coriander**, to garnish

Vegetable jalfrezi is a fabulous, fairly fiery vegan main course, or a super-quick spicy side.

Heat the oil in a large frying pan or wok with a lid, set over a medium-high heat. When hot, add the onion and cook for 5 minutes, until softened.

Meanwhile, mix all the ground spices together in a bowl.

Add the tomato purée to the frying pan, stir to coat the onions and cook for about 2 minutes. Add all the vegetables and the mixed spices and stir-fry for 3–4 minutes – we like the vegetables to have a lot of bite. Add some salt and pepper and the water, mix well and cover with the lid. Let steam for a further 3 minutes, until the vegetables are just tender but still have a crisp bite.

Serve with naan and scattered with the fresh coriander.

This is a great way of using up small quantities of stray vegetables in the fridge – a lonely carrot or a solitary pepper. Use this as a guide and add anything from mushrooms to courgettes to frozen peas.

SMOKY CURRY-SPICED LAMB CHOPS

SERVES 4

PREP TIME: 10 MINS, PLUS OPTIONAL 4 HOURS MARINATING • COOK TIME: 6 MINS

WF • GF • NF • SoF

2 cloves of **garlic**, crushed

3cm piece of **ginger**, peeled and finely grated

1 teaspoon **ground cumin**

1 teaspoon **ground coriander**

½ teaspoon **hot chilli powder**

1 teaspoon **sweet smoked paprika**

1 tablespoon **full-fat plain yoghurt**

1 teaspoon **freshly squeezed lemon** or **lime juice**

a really generous pinch of **salt** and some **freshly ground black pepper**

4–8 (depending on their size and your hunger) thick **lamb chops**

TO SERVE:

Choose one or two of the following:

Dhal (pages 26, 79, or 135)

Raita (pages 163–4)

Tamarind Yoghurt (page 165)

Kachumber Salad (page 192)

Koshambari Salad (page 191)

rice or **Indian flatbreads** (pages 198–201 and 205–6)

For an altogether more interesting take on meat-and-two-veg, serve these chops with Sag Paneer (page 60), Dhal (pages 26, 79 or 135) and some Bombay Potatoes (page 187).

In a large bowl, mix together all the ingredients, except the chops, until well combined. Add the chops and rub the marinade all over the meat, working it in with your fingers. If possible, leave to marinate for 4 hours or so, but you can cook immediately, if you want.

Whack the grill up to its highest setting and wait for it to get really hot.

Shake or scrape any excess marinade from the chops – you want a little coating the meat, but not so much that the meat is wet, as it won't brown. Cook the chops under the very hot grill for 2–3 minutes per side, or until the marinade is sizzling and the edges of the fat are beginning to brown, and the meat is cooked to your liking – we like it pink. (Exactly how long depends on the power of your grill and the thickness of the chops.)

Serve with one or two of the suggested accompaniments.

≡ TIP ≡

We cook this under the grill as the marinade is less likely to burn, but feel free to cook these in a very hot griddle pan, or on the BBQ, where you'll get more tasty char.

CURRY-SPICED TOFU

SERVES 4
PREP TIME: 15 MINS, PLUS OPTIONAL 10–30 MINS MARINATING • COOK TIME: 30 MINS
WF • GF • DF • V • VE • NF

400g **extra-firm tofu**, cut into 2–3cm
    slices, about 1cm thick
1 clove of **garlic**, crushed
1 teaspoon peeled and finely grated
    ginger
½ teaspoon **ground cumin**
¼ teaspoon **ground coriander**
¼ teaspoon **ground turmeric**
a pinch of **ground cinnamon**
a pinch of **hot chilli powder** (optional)
1 teaspoon **soy sauce**
1 teaspoon **neutral cooking oil**, plus extra
    for greasing
a pinch of **salt** and **freshly ground**
    black pepper

These little nuggets of tofu work brilliantly on top of vegetarian curries.

Line a plate or chopping board with 2 sheets of kitchen paper and arrange the tofu in a single layer on top. Cover with more kitchen paper and use your hands or another board or plate to gently press out as much liquid as you can – this will result in crisper tofu when cooked.

Mix together the remaining ingredients to form a paste. Spread this on the top and bottom of each slice of tofu. If you have time, leave to marinate for 10–30 minutes, but you can cook immediately, if wished.

When ready to cook, heat the oven to 200°C/400°F/gas mark 6. Line a baking sheet with baking paper and brush it with a little oil.

Place the tofu on the baking sheet and bake for 30 minutes, turning once halfway through, until golden brown. Serve immediately.

TIP

Mustard oil adds a peppery, earthy
note to this, so you could drizzle over
a little just before serving.

THAI-SPICED TOFU

SERVES 4

PREP TIME: 10 MINS, PLUS OPTIONAL 10–30 MINS MARINATING • COOK TIME: 8 MINS

WF • GF • DF • V • VE (if made without fish sauce; also check curry and chilli paste ingredients) • NF

400g **extra-firm tofu**, cut into 2–3cm slices, about 1cm thick

2 tablespoons good-quality **Thai red curry paste** (choose a vegan brand if necessary, or use the recipe on page 43, omitting the fish sauce)

neutral cooking oil

salt, to taste

TO DRESS:

freshly squeezed **lime juice**

fish sauce

Thai Sriracha hot sauce

Thai chilli paste (nam prik pao; check for shrimp paste, if V or Ve)

chilli oil

sesame oil

This is a great way to add extra protein to a vegan curry, as well as adding flavour to notoriously bland tofu. Use it to top any Thai curry or in a Thai main dish, in place of meat or fish.

Line a plate or chopping board with 2 sheets of kitchen paper and arrange the tofu in a single layer on top. Cover with more kitchen paper and use your hands or another board or plate to gently press out as much liquid as you can – this will result in crisper tofu when cooked.

Use your hands to gently rub the Thai red curry paste over and into each slice of tofu. If you have time, leave to marinate for 10–30 minutes, but you can cook immediately, if wished.

Heat a 1cm depth of oil in a non-stick frying pan set over a medium-low heat. When hot, slide in the tofu slices (work in batches if necessary) and cook, fairly gently, for about 4 minutes on each side, until the tofu is golden and beginning to crisp up and the curry paste is dark red, but not scorched. Repeat until all the slices have been cooked, keeping the cooked slices warm.

Season with a little salt and dress with one or two of the suggested options, to fit whatever you are serving it with.

= TIP =

Be sure your brand of tofu is firm – the silky, wobbly kind won't work here.

SRI LANKAN-STYLE GREEN BEAN & COURGETTE CURRY

SERVES 4
PREP TIME: 15 MINS • COOK TIME: 20 MINS
WF • GF • DF • V • VE • NF • SoF

200g **shallots**, finely sliced

2 teaspoons finely chopped **green chilli**

600g **courgette**, sliced into ½cm pieces

300g **long green beans**, trimmed

1 teaspoon **ground turmeric**

a generous pinch of **fenugreek seeds**

10 **curry leaves**

600ml **full-fat coconut milk**

¼–½ teaspoon **salt**, or to taste

¼ teaspoon **hot chilli powder** or **cayenne pepper**, or to taste

rice or **Indian flatbreads** (pages 198–201 and 205–6), to serve

FOR THE ROASTED CURRY POWDER GARNISH:

½ teaspoon **uncooked rice**

¼ teaspoon each **black mustard**, **coriander**, **cumin** and **fennel seeds**

a pinch of **fenugreek seeds**

¼ teaspoon **dried red chilli flakes**

2 **cloves**

seeds from 3 **green cardamom pods**

4 **curry leaves**

¼ teaspoon **ground turmeric**

This simple pale-yellow curry is often served very hot and spicy in Sri Lanka, so feel free to ramp up the chilli content for a more authentic version. The roasted Sri Lankan curry powder isn't essential, but lasts well if sealed in a jar.

First make the roasted curry powder garnish, if using: heat a dry frying pan over a medium heat. When hot, add the rice and mustards seeds and, when the seeds start to crackle, add all the other ingredients, except the turmeric. Cook, stirring constantly, for 3–5 minutes, until well toasted – the aim is to get the mixture off the heat just before the spices burn. Remove from the heat and stir the turmeric into the pan, then tip everything out into a pestle and mortar and grind to a powder. Set aside.

Place all the ingredients for the curry, except the chilli powder or cayenne pepper, into a large pan with a lid. Stir well to ensure the spices are mixed into the coconut milk and the courgette is well coated, and press the vegetables down into the liquid. Place the pan over a low heat, cover and slowly bring to a simmer (don't rush, as the coconut milk may split). Simmer gently for 10 minutes, stirring once or twice, until the courgette is just tender and the beans still have some bite (check after 6 minutes or so, to ensure the vegetables aren't cooking too fast). Taste to check salt levels, and add the chilli powder or cayenne pepper.

Serve in wide bowls, sprinkled with a pinch of the roasted curry powder, if using, with flatbreads or rice.

TIP

Although delish on its own, Sri Lankans often eat a range of curry dishes and sides together, so you could serve this with dhal (page 26, 79 or 135) and a meat or fish curry, as well.

=≡ TIP ≡=

Any mixture of
seafood, including
shellfish, will work here —
just cook, lid on, for 3–4
minutes, until the shells
pop open.

BURMESE-STYLE FISH, PRAWN & TOMATO CURRY

SERVES 2
PREP TIME: 20 MINS • COOK TIME: 20 MINS
WF • GF • DF • NF • SoF

2 teaspoons **ground turmeric**

¼–½ teaspoon **cayenne pepper**

1 tablespoon **fish sauce**, or more to taste

400g **firm white fish** or **salmon**, cut into 3cm chunks

2 **onions**, roughly diced

3 cloves of **garlic**, roughly chopped

4cm piece of **ginger**, peeled and roughly chopped

½–1 medium **red chilli** (deseeded to taste), roughly chopped

2 tablespoons **neutral cooking oil**

500g **fresh tomatoes**, blitzed until smooth in a food processor (or 400g **canned chopped tomatoes** or **passata**)

2 teaspoons **sweet paprika**

300g **raw prawns**, peeled (deveined if you prefer)

a generous pinch of **dried red chilli flakes** (optional)

1 tablespoon **freshly squeezed lime juice**, plus 4 **lime wedges**

a large handful of **fresh coriander**, roughly chopped

steamed rice, to serve

A simple – but brilliantly tasty – curry, this is a spin on a recipe Rebecca found in the wonderful book **Share,** *by Alison Oakervee, a collection of uplifting recipes from war-torn countries, with the non-profit organization Women for Women International.*

In a large bowl, mix the turmeric, cayenne and fish sauce to a paste, add the fish and toss to thoroughly coat in the mixture. Cover and set aside.

In a small blender, blitz the onions, garlic, ginger and chilli to a coarse purée, scraping down the sides with a spatula. (Alternatively, use a pestle and mortar.)

Heat the oil in a large deep pan with a lid over a medium heat. When hot, add the onion mixture and cook for about 10 minutes, stirring frequently, until translucent and beginning to brown. Add the tomatoes and bring to a simmer. Stir in the paprika, reduce the heat to low and simmer for 5 minutes, or until the raw flavour of the tomatoes disappears – taste to be sure. (If using canned tomatoes and the sauce seems dry, add a little water to the pan and bring back to a simmer.) Add the fish and marinade, cover and cook for 3 minutes, then gently stir and taste. Add more fish sauce for saltiness, or the chilli flakes for more heat.

Next, push the prawns into the curry. Cook for 1–2 minutes, until pink. Remove from the heat, add the lime juice and most of the chopped coriander. Stir once, being careful not to break up the fish too much.

Serve with steamed rice, sprinkled with the remaining coriander and with lime wedges to squeeze over.

RAJMA

SERVES 2 AS A MAIN OR 4 WITH OTHER DISHES
PREP TIME: 10 MINS • COOK TIME: 28 MINS
WF • GF • V • VE • DF (if using vegan ghee) **• NF • SoF • SUITABLE FOR FREEZING**

1 tablespoon **neutral cooking oil**

1 **onion**, finely chopped

2 cloves of **garlic**, crushed

3cm piece of **ginger**, peeled and grated

1 medium **green chilli**, deseeded and finely chopped

1½ tablespoons **tomato purée**

6 **green cardamom pods**

¼ teaspoon **ground cinnamon**

¼ teaspoon **ground cumin**

½ teaspoon **ground coriander**

a pinch of **hot chilli powder** (or less, to taste)

½ teaspoon **garam masala**

400g **canned cooked kidney beans in water**, undrained

1 **bay leaf**

a pinch of **sugar**

a knob of **butter** or **ghee** (optional but magical) (ghee can be vegan)

a handful of **fresh coriander**

salt and **freshly ground black pepper**

steamed rice or **Naan** (see page 198), to serve

This incredibly restorative kidney bean curry is usually served with rice but we often serve it with some fluffy naan to create a northern Indian equivalent of beans on toast.

Heat the oil in a medium saucepan over a medium heat. Add the onion and cook for about 8 minutes, stirring often, until just beginning to brown.

Reduce the heat to low, add the garlic, ginger and chilli and cook for 2 minutes, stirring. Stir in the tomato purée and cook for 3 minutes, stirring to prevent the mixture sticking. Add all the spices and continue to stir for 1 minute (don't let the mixture catch and burn or the spices will become bitter). Add the kidney beans, along with the water from the can, bay leaf, sugar and some salt and pepper. Fill the can one-third full with water, then pour that into the pan, too. Increase the heat and bring to the boil, then reduce the heat and simmer for 15 minutes, stirring now and then.

Remove from the heat and stir through the knob of butter or ghee, if using, and taste for salt and pepper. Remove and discard the bay leaf and cardamom pods, if you can find them, then stir through the coriander leaves.

Serve with steamed rice or warm naan.

= TIP =

For a posh dinner party or restaurant-style touch, add 3 tablespoons of cream just before serving.

FISH BHUNA

SERVES 4

PREP TIME: 18 MINS • COOK TIME: 35 MINS, PLUS 5 MINS STANDING

WF • GF • DF • NF • SoF

1 tablespoon **neutral cooking oil**

1 **onion**, finely sliced

2 cloves of **garlic**, crushed

3cm piece of **ginger**, peeled and finely grated

6 **green cardamom pods**, bruised

¼ teaspoon **fennel seeds**

¼ teaspoon **ground turmeric**

¼ teaspoon **hot chilli powder**

½ teaspoon **garam masala**

½ teaspoon **ground coriander**

150ml **water**, plus extra as needed

1 tablespoon **tomato purée**

2 medium **tomatoes**, deseeded, cored and very finely chopped

4 fillets of any **firm white fish**, each cut into 2 or 3 large pieces

a pinch of **salt**

lemon wedges, to serve

Hold your nerve when cooking the spices for this – they need some intense pan-roasting (although, don't burn 'em). The sauce should be thick enough to coat the fish, when cooked.

Heat the oil in a large pan with a lid, set over a medium heat. Add the onions and cook for about 8–10 minutes, stirring, until they begin to brown. Add the garlic and ginger and sizzle for 30 seconds. Mix all the spices together with a pinch of salt, then add to the pan and cook for 1½ minutes, until fragrant and almost – but not quite – burning.

Add the water and simmer until the water is almost entirely evaporated, about 10 minutes, leaving a thick paste with an oily sheen. Add the tomato purée and fresh tomatoes to the pan and cook gently until the tomatoes have softened, about 6–8 minutes. Add the fish to the pan, along with 1 or 2 tablespoons of water – just enough to stop everything sticking, but not so much that the gravy becomes at all saucy. Reduce the heat to low, cover and let the fish part-fry, part-steam in the pan for about 5 minutes.

Remove from the heat, uncover, very gently stir once and leave to stand for 5 minutes before serving.

≡ TIP ≡

This also works with boneless chicken, cut into strips, but you will need to increase the cooking time a little.

GYM BUNNY CURRY

SERVES 4

PREP TIME: 15 MINS • COOK TIME: 45 MINS

DF • V WF • GF (if served with rice) • **NF • SoF** (if using NF or SoF yoghurt)

4 **eggs**

1 tablespoon **neutral cooking oil**

4 **curry leaves**, torn

½ teaspoon **cumin seeds**

1 **onion**, finely diced

3cm piece of **ginger**, peeled and finely grated

1 clove of **garlic**, crushed

1 **red chilli**, finely chopped

6 **green cardamom pods**

1 teaspoon **ground turmeric**

1 teaspoon **ground coriander**

400g **canned chopped tomatoes**, undrained

5 tablespoons **full-fat coconut milk** (or **full-fat plain yoghurt** or **non-dairy yoghurt**)

a handful of **fresh coriander**, to serve

rice or **Indian flatbreads** (pages 198–201 and 205–6), to serve

TIP

This is a good lunchbox curry – cook the eggs in the morning, then take to work in their shells. Peel and warm everything up together.

A high-protein curry, perfect post workout. No bunnies involved.

Place the eggs in a deep saucepan with a lid and cover with water by about 2cm. Set over a high heat and bring to a fast boil, then remove from the heat, cover with a lid and let stand for 8 minutes. Use tongs to remove the eggs from the pan, then cool under cold running water. Peel and set aside.

Heat the oil in a large pan set over a medium heat. Add the curry leaves and cumin seeds and sizzle for 2 minutes, then add the onion and cook for about 8 minutes, stirring, until translucent. Add the ginger, garlic, chilli, cardamom, turmeric and ground coriander and cook, stirring, for about 5 minutes, or until it forms an oily-looking paste and smells delicious. Add the tomatoes and 100ml water, then stir well, scraping any paste up from the bottom of the pan, and bring to a simmer.

Reduce the heat to low and cook for up to 30 minutes, squashing any lumps of tomato with the back of a spoon, until it is thick, tart and spicy, and the raw flavour of the tomatoes has completely disappeared (add a splash of water if the pan gets too dry).

Remove from the heat and stir in the coconut milk and half the coriander. Cut the eggs in half and place in the hot curry, to warm through. Serve with the rest of the coriander scattered on top with rice or Indian flatbreads.

DORO ALICHA TIBS

SERVES 4
PREP TIME: 20 MINS • COOK TIME: 30 MINS
WF • GF • NF • SoF

2 tablespoons **neutral cooking oil**

1 large **onion**, diced

2cm piece of **ginger**, peeled and grated

2 cloves of **garlic**, crushed

1 tablespoon **paprika**

a generous pinch of **ground cardamom**

a generous pinch of **ground cinnamon**

600g **chicken breast** and boneless **thighs**, chopped into small pieces

a generous pinch of **salt**

1 **plum tomato**, diced

hot green chillies, deseeded and thinly sliced, to garnish

rice and **salad**, **cooked long green beans** or **cabbage**, to serve

Every Friday, the team at the LEON support office in London descends on a nearby street food stall, Ethiopian Flavours, where chefs cook up Ethiopian curries, vegetables and rice. The owner, Davide Ghetaceu, gave us his recipe for home-cooked doro alicha tibs, an Ethiopian chicken curry. Simple to make, it is incredibly tasty.

Heat the oil in a large saucepan over a medium heat, then add the onion and sauté for 8–10 minutes, until golden. Reduce the heat, add the ginger, garlic, paprika, cardamom and cinnamon and cook until well combined, about 2 minutes.

Add the chicken along with a good pinch of salt and stir until well coated in the spices. Increase the heat to medium-high and cook for about 10 minutes, stirring, until the chicken is browned and well-sealed all over.

Add the tomato, reduce the heat to low and cook, stirring often, for about 10 minutes or until the chicken is cooked through. Towards the end of cooking, if the pan is very dry, add a splash of water, but bear in mind this is a relatively dry curry.

Sprinkle with the sliced green chillies, and serve with rice, a salad, cooked green beans or cabbage.

= TIP =

If you don't have ground cardamom, pop the seeds out of 4 green cardamom pods and grind to a powder in a pestle and mortar.

CURRIED PRAWN STIR-FRY

SERVES 4 WITH OTHER DISHES
PREP TIME: 20 MINS • COOK TIME: 20 MINS
WF • GF • DF • NF • SoF

FOR THE CURRY POWDER:

seeds from 4 **green cardamom pods**

2 **cloves**

¼ teaspoon **fennel seeds**

¼ teaspoon **cumin seeds**

¼ teaspoon **coriander seeds**

¼ teaspoon **ground turmeric**

¼ teaspoon **ground cinnamon**

¼ teaspoon **dried red chilli flakes**

FOR THE CURRY:

1 tablespoon **neutral cooking oil**

1 **onion**, finely sliced

1 clove of **garlic**, crushed

1 teaspoon peeled and finely grated
 ginger

6 **curry leaves**

1 **green chilli** (deseeded or not, to taste),
 finely chopped

1 teaspoon **tomato purée**

500g **large prawns** (fresh, or frozen and
 defrosted), peeled

a drop of **tamarind paste** or **concentrate**

salt, to taste

Loosely inspired by prawn curries found in Malaysia and Indonesia, this stir-fried dry curry can also be turned into a soupy coconut curry – just add 200ml of coconut milk after the curry powder and bring up to a simmer, then add some salt, as needed.

Place all the curry powder ingredients in a pestle and mortar or spice grinder and pummel to a fine powder. Set aside.

Heat the oil in a wide frying pan over a medium heat. Add the onion, and sauté for about 8 minutes, until the onion begins to brown. Add a pinch of salt, the garlic, ginger, curry leaves, green chilli and tomato purée and cook for 5 minutes, stirring constantly. Add the curry powder and cook for 1 minute, then add the prawns and tamarind and sauté for 5 minutes, or until the prawns are pink, cooked through and well coated in the spice mixture.

Remove from the heat and serve immediately.

= TIP =

For a vegan version, omit the prawns and cook 2–3 diced aubergines along with the onion, adding a splash of water towards the end of cooking if the pan seems very dry.

≡ TIP ≡

Don't use jackfruit
in syrup by mistake – the
can (or, occasionally, packet)
must say 'young' or 'unripe
green jackfruit in brine' or
'water'.

SRI LANKAN-STYLE JACKFRUIT CURRY

· ·

SERVES 4
PREP TIME: 20 MINS • COOK TIME: 45 MINS
WF • GF • DF • V • Ve • NF • SoF

· ·

1 tablespoon **neutral cooking oil**, plus
  a splash

2 **onions**, 1 finely sliced and 1 finely diced

1½ teaspoons **mustard seeds**

10 **curry leaves**, divided

a generous pinch of dried **red chilli flakes**

a generous pinch of **cumin seeds**

400g **canned unripe green jackfruit**,
  drained and rinsed

3cm piece of **ginger**, peeled and grated

2 cloves of **garlic**, crushed

1 **green chilli**, finely chopped

½ teaspoon **ground turmeric**

¼ teaspoon **cayenne pepper**

300g **cauliflower**, broken into florets

400ml **full-fat coconut milk**

½ teaspoon **tamarind paste**

a pinch of **sugar**

125g **long green beans**, trimmed

125g **okra**, trimmed and sliced into 1cm
  pieces (optional)

½–1 teaspoon **Sri Lankan roasted curry
  powder** (see page 106) or **hot Madras
  curry powder**

salt and **freshly ground black pepper**

rice or **Indian flatbreads** (pages 198–201
  and 205–6), to serve

We only discovered jackfruit when we wrote our **Fast Vegan** *cookbook, because the unripe green fruit (sold ready-cooked in cans or packets) is an amazing meat substitute. We do feel a* **tiny** *bit silly: Southeast Asian, especially Sri Lankan, cooks have been using it for centuries.*

· ·

Heat 1 tablespoon oil in a large heavy-based pan with a lid over a medium heat. Add the sliced onion and sauté for 10 minutes, until starting to brown. Add 1 teaspoon of the mustard seeds, the curry leaves, chilli flakes and cumin seeds and cook for a further 5 minutes. The onions should be well browned and the mustard seeds should start to crackle. Remove from the heat, scrape into a bowl and set aside.

Meanwhile, prepare the jackfruit. Discard the woody core and any large seeds, and shred the softer flesh. Set aside.

Add a splash more oil to the pan with the chopped onion and cook for 8 minutes, until translucent, then add the ginger, garlic, green chilli and remaining mustard seeds. Cook for 5 minutes, stirring (the mustard seeds should pop as before), then add the turmeric and cayenne. Cook for 1 minute, reduce the heat and add the cauliflower, jackfruit, coconut milk, tamarind paste, sugar and some salt and pepper. Slowly bring to a simmer and cook for 10 minutes.

Add the green beans and okra, if using, along with ½ teaspoon of curry powder. Mix well, then cover and cook for 5 minutes, until the vegetables are crisp-tender, apart from the jackfruit, which should be melting into the sauce. Remove from the heat. Stir about one-third of the tempered onions through the curry, then taste and add a little more salt, pepper, cayenne or roasted curry powder, as needed. Serve topped with the remaining tempered onions, with rice or Indian flatbreads.

THAI-STYLE CLAM CURRY

SERVES 4

PREP TIME: 15 MINS • COOK TIME: 17 MINS

WF • GF • DF • NF • SoF

1 tablespoon **neutral cooking oil**

1 **onion**, finely sliced

a pinch of **salt**

1 stick of **lemongrass**, outer layer and hard stem removed, finely chopped

2 cloves of **garlic**, crushed

2 **red chillies**, finely chopped

2 heaped teaspoons **nam prik pao** (Thai roasted chilli paste)

400ml **full-fat coconut milk**

2 teaspoons **fish sauce**, or more to taste

6 **lime leaves**, torn

½ teaspoon **tamarind paste** or **concentrate**

1kg **fresh live clams**

a handful of **Thai basil leaves** (optional)

lime wedges, to serve (optional)

steamed rice or **Thai noodles**, to serve

═ TIP ═

If you want to add vegetables, use sliced baby corn, canned bamboo shoots, fine ribbons of carrot, shredded greens or finely sliced peppers. They can all be added at the same time as the lemongrass and garlic.

Nam prik pao, a Thai roasted chilli paste, is a powerhouse of an ingredient and is now widely available. Use it on its own to add a wallop of flavour to stir-fries, or mix with coconut milk in curries.

Heat the oil in a large heavy-based pan with a lid, set over a medium heat. Add the onion and salt and cook for about 8 minutes, until softened. Add the lemongrass, garlic and chilli, and cook for 1 minute, then add the nam prik pao and stir well. Shake the can of coconut milk well then add to the mixture with the fish sauce, lime leaves and tamarind (be careful not to add too much tamarind as it will overwhelm everything, given the chance). Gently bring up to a simmer, then taste – the broth should be spicy, savoury and tangy. Add more fish sauce, if needed, remembering that the clams will bring their own salty-sweetness in a moment.

Increase the heat and bring the curry to a merry simmer. Tip the clams into the pan and cover with the lid. Cook for 3½ minutes, giving the pan a firm jiggle once or twice. Remove the lid and discard any clams that have remained closed. Stir through half of the Thai basil leaves, if using.

Serve the clams and their wonderful curry broth in shallow bowls, with rice or noodles on the side. Top with the rest of the Thai basil leaves and give each diner a wedge of lime to squeeze over, and a spoon.

AUBERGINE AND TOMATO CURRY

2 medium **aubergines**

1 tablespoon **neutral cooking oil**

2 cloves of **garlic**, crushed

3cm piece of **ginger**, peeled and finely grated

1 **green chilli** (deseeded or not, to taste), finely chopped

1 teaspoon **ground cumin**

1 teaspoon **ground coriander**

1 teaspoon **ground turmeric**

¼–½ teaspoon **hot chilli powder**, to taste

1 teaspoon **fennel seeds**

400g **canned chopped tomatoes**, undrained

150ml **water**

a generous pinch of **sugar**

salt and **freshly ground black pepper**

a handful of **fresh coriander**

Very, very easy and very, very tasty.

Trim the aubergines, then cut in half crossways through the middle. Cut into finger-sized wedges and trim any seedy parts of the flesh (otherwise they will expand during cooking and you will end up with threads of seeds trailing through the finished curry).

Heat the oil in a large saucepan with a lid, set over a medium heat. When hot, add the garlic, ginger and chilli and cook, stirring, for 3 minutes. Stir in the cumin, coriander, turmeric, chilli powder and fennel seeds and gently cook for 2 minutes, then add the tomatoes, water, aubergine wedges, sugar and a pinch of salt and some freshly ground black pepper. Push the aubergines into the liquid, then cover with the lid, bring up to a merry simmer and cook for about 15 minutes.

Remove the lid – the aubergines will have collapsed into the curry. Increase the heat a little and let the sauce reduce for about 10 minutes.

Remove from the heat and check that the aubergines are meltingly tender, then stir through the coriander leaves before serving.

= TIP =

Bulk this out by adding cooked chickpeas, cubes of paneer or firm tofu, or roasted peppers from a jar (in oil).

SLOW

LAMB ROGAN JOSH

SERVES 4

PREP TIME: 10 MINS, PLUS 20 MINS–8 HOURS MARINATING • COOK TIME: 50 MINS

WF • GF • DF (if substituting the yoghurt) • **NF** (if using dairy yoghurt) • **SoF • SUITABLE FOR FREEZING**

800g boneless **lamb shoulder**, cut into bite-sized chunks, fat trimmed

5 heaped tablespoons **full-fat plain yoghurt** (or a non-dairy yoghurt)

4cm piece of **ginger**, peeled and finely grated

½ teaspoon **chilli powder**

2 teaspoons **paprika**

a generous pinch of **salt**

1 tablespoon **neutral cooking oil**

¼ teaspoon **ground mace**

½ teaspoon **asafoetida**

5 **cloves**

seeds from 4 **green cardamom pods**

½ teaspoon **fennel seeds**

a generous grinding of **black pepper**

a pinch of **saffron**

250ml **hot water**

rice, to serve (optional)

a small handful of **fresh coriander**, to garnish (optional)

≡ TIP ≡

If you can get your hands on brilliant brick-red Kashmiri chilli powder, which is pretty mild, use it instead of our paprika-and-chilli mix.

We wanted this recipe to be close to the Kashmiri original, which doesn't contain onions, garlic or tomatoes. You do need the asafoetida powder to give it an onion-y flavour; if you don't have any, soften a finely chopped onion in the oil for 10 minutes before adding the lamb. (This recipe is loosely based on one by the brilliant food writer Maunika Gowardhan.)

Place the lamb in a bowl with the yoghurt, ginger, chilli powder and paprika and a generous pinch of salt. Mix to coat the lamb, then marinate in the fridge for at least 20 minutes, although overnight is even better.

Heat the oil in a large deep pan set over a medium heat. When hot, add the lamb and its marinade, and cook until the lamb is lightly browned all over and the marinade has reduced, about 8–10 minutes.

Meanwhile, place all the spices in a pestle and mortar or a spice grinder and grind until smooth and well combined.

Reduce the heat to low and add the spices to the pan. Cook, stirring often, for about 10 minutes, until really fragrant.

Meanwhile, soak the saffron in the hot water for about 5 minutes, then pour the mixture into the pan. Bring up to a gentle simmer, then cover and gently cook for about 20 minutes.

Finally, remove the lid and let the gravy (which should be quite thin even at the end of cooking) reduce by about half; about a further 10 minutes.

Serve with rice and sprinkled with the fresh coriander leaves, if liked.

≡ TIP ≡

A version of this is made with waxy potatoes cooked in the curry, which is irresistible.

BEEF RENDANG

1 tablespoon **neutral cooking oil**

1½ tablespoons **tamarind paste**

2 **cloves**

3 **green cardamom pods**

2cm stick of **cinnamon**

1 teaspoon **sugar**

800g **beef shin**, cut into chunks

400ml **full-fat coconut milk**

100ml **water**

1 stalk **lemongrass**, bruised

5 **lime leaves**, roughly torn

4½ tablespoons **desiccated coconut**

dried red chilli flakes, to taste

salt, to taste

FOR THE CURRY PASTE:

1 large **onion**, finely chopped

4 cloves of **garlic**, crushed

1 stalk **lemongrass**, outer layer removed, finely chopped

4cm piece of **ginger**, peeled and grated

1 teaspoon **galangal paste**, or peeled and very finely chopped **fresh galangal**

2–3 small **dried red chillies**, crumbled

1 **fresh red chilli**, deseeded and finely chopped

a generous pinch of **salt**

This incredible slow-cooked beef curry is associated with both Indonesia and Malaysia – in fact, John was taught how to make it by a fantastic cook called Chef Ann in Malaysia, while on holiday with Katie and their kids (Chef Ann's recipes also appear in our Family & Friends *cookbook). The scent of it cooking is almost as good as the eating.*

Use a small blender or pestle and mortar to grind the curry paste ingredients until fairly smooth. Add 1 tablespoon of water if needed to loosen the mixture.

Heat the oil in a large, heavy-based pan with a lid, set over a low-medium heat. When hot, add the curry paste and fry for 3 minutes, stirring constantly, until fragrant and sizzling. Add the tamarind concentrate, cloves, cardamom pods, cinnamon stick and sugar and continue to fry for another 5 minutes.

Add the beef, coconut milk, water, lemongrass, lime leaves and a generous pinch of salt, gently bring up to a simmer (so that the coconut milk doesn't split), then cover and cook for 2½–3 hours, until the beef is meltingly tender and the sauce has reduced to a dark brown, thick gravy.

About 10 minutes before serving, place a dry frying pan over a medium heat. When hot, add the desiccated coconut and toast, stirring constantly, until golden, being sure to toss the coconut enough that the bottom flakes don't burn. Stir the coconut into the curry.

Taste and add more salt or dried red chilli flakes, as needed. Serve with plain steamed or coconut rice (see page 168), with some garlicky sautéd greens on the side.

LAMB DHANSAK

SERVES 4

PREP TIME: 25 MINS • COOK TIME: 2 HOURS

WF • GF • DF • NF • SoF • SUITABLE FOR FREEZING

75g **split white urid/urad dal lentils** (optional)

50g (or 125g) **yellow split peas**

50g **split red lentils**

½ teaspoon **coriander seeds**

¼ teaspoon **cumin seeds**

seeds from 3 **green cardamom pods**

3 **cloves**

½ teaspoon **fennel seeds**

a pinch of **fenugreek seeds**

¼ teaspoon **ground cinnamon**

½ teaspoon **ground turmeric**

a pinch of **freshly grated nutmeg**

a pinch of **freshly ground black pepper**

1 tablespoon **neutral cooking oil**

2 **onions**, finely chopped

4 cloves of **garlic**, crushed or finely grated

4cm piece of **ginger**, peeled and finely grated

750g **lamb shoulder**, diced

100g **fresh tomatoes**, chopped

1 tablespoon each **finely chopped green chilli**, **fresh dill**, **fresh mint** and **fresh coriander**

1 tablespoon **tamarind paste**

50g **frozen fenugreek leaves** (optional)

up to ½ teaspoon **salt**, or to taste

Traditionally, this Parsi lamb and lentil stew is made with toor dal (pigeon peas), but split peas are easier to find.

Wash the lentils and pick over for debris. Place in a large lidded pan with 1 litre of hot water and bring to a fast boil. Boil for 5 minutes, skimming off any scum, then reduce the heat, cover and simmer for 25 minutes.

Use a pestle and mortar or spice grinder to grind the whole spices, then mix together with the ground spices. Set aside. Heat the oven to 140°C/275°F/gas mark 1.

Heat the oil in a large deep, ovenproof pan with a lid over a medium heat. Add the onions and cook for 10 minutes, stirring often, until slightly browned. Add the garlic, ginger and spice mixture and cook for 2 minutes, stirring. Add the lamb and cook, stirring, for 5 minutes, until slightly browned. Add the tomatoes and cook for 5 minutes, stirring now and then. Add the chilli, herbs (saving a little of each herb to garnish), tamarind and fenugreek leaves, if using.

Ladle the lentils into the onion pan. If it seems dry, add a little water. Bring to a simmer, then cover and cook in the oven for 1 hour. Check the lamb at this point and return to the oven for 15–30 minutes as necessary – you want it to be falling apart.

To thicken the gravy, scoop 4 ladles of the lentils, vegetables and broth (leaving the meat in the pan) into a food processor and blitz until smooth, then return to the pan. If it still seems a little thin, place on the heat and simmer to reduce.

Add ¼ teaspoon of salt, then taste to see if you want more (or more chilli for heat, or tamarind for sourness). Serve, sprinkled with the remaining herbs, with rice or Indian flatbreads (see pages 198–201 and 205–6).

= TIP =

If you prefer, you can make this in one pot, but lentil cooking times can be unpredictable when mixed with other things, so we like to get them started on their own. Try adding diced aubergine or squash along with the onion, or add a handful of finely chopped spinach 5 minutes before serving.

TIP

Urid/urad dal is easy to find in Asian supermarkets and online – just make sure you choose the black variety for this dish, rather than the white.

BLACK DHAL MAKHANI

SERVES 4
PREP TIME: 15 MINS, PLUS 8 HOURS SOAKING • COOK TIME: 6 HOURS
WF • GF • V • NF • SoF (check flatbreads) • SUITABLE FOR FREEZING

200g **dried black lentils** (urid/urad dal), soaked for 8 hours or overnight in cold water, drained and rinsed

3 teaspoons of **butter** or **ghee**

5 **cloves**

4 **green cardamom pods**

¼ teaspoon **fennel seeds**

½ teaspoon **cumin seeds**

1 teaspoon **garam masala**

¼ teaspoon **ground cinnamon**

¼ teaspoon **chilli powder**

3cm piece of **ginger**, peeled and finely grated

2 cloves of **garlic**, crushed

½ **green chilli**, deseeded and finely chopped

1 **onion**, finely chopped

1 tablespoon **tomato purée**

1 **bay leaf**

1 teaspoon **brown sugar**

100g (½ can) **canned cooked kidney beans**, drained and rinsed

4 tablespoons **double cream**

salt, to taste

a handful of **fresh coriander**, to garnish

poppadoms or **Indian flatbreads** (see pages 198–201 and 205–6), to serve

Don't be put off by the length of time this Punjabi dhal takes to make – you barely need to look at it once it's cooking and it really, truly, is worth the wait. We wrote this recipe for **LEON** Happy Soups *a few years ago – our own version of the famous Dishoom classic.*

Place the lentils and 750ml hot water in a non-reactive pan with a lid, bring to a fast boil and cook for 5 minutes. Skim off any scum, reduce the heat, cover and cook for 30–40 minutes, until the lentils are soft and beginning to break down.

Melt 1 teaspoon of the butter or ghee in a large ovenproof saucepan with a lid, set over a low heat. Add the cardamom pods, fennel, cumin, garam masala, cinnamon and chilli powder. Cook, stirring, for 2 minutes, then add the ginger and garlic, and cook for 1–2 minutes. Add 1 more teaspoon of butter, the green chilli, onion, a pinch of salt and the tomato purée and cook for about 10 minutes, stirring often, until the onion is soft. Remove from the heat, add the bay leaf and sugar, and set aside.

Heat the oven to 140°C/275°F/gas mark 1.

Roughly mash the kidney beans and add to the onion pan. Ladle the lentils and their cooking liquid into the same pan, then cover and cook in the oven for 4–5 hours, or longer if you can, adding 3–4 tablespoons of water every hour, and stirring the contents of the pan to prevent sticking.

When ready, the dhal will be very creamy and, the longer you leave it, the deeper brown it will be. Remove from the oven and stir in the cream and the remaining butter, plus enough hot water to loosen it to a thick soup. Taste and add a little more salt, if necessary. Remove the bay leaf and cardamom pods. Garnish with fresh coriander and eat with poppadoms or wedges of Indian flatbreads for dunking.

BUTTERNUT, CHICKPEA & KALE CURRY

SERVES 4

PREP TIME: 25 MINS • COOK TIME: 55 MINS

WF • GF • DF • V • Ve • NF • SoF

2 tablespoons **neutral cooking oil**

1 teaspoon **mustard seeds**

2 teaspoons **cumin seeds**

1 teaspoon **dried red chilli flakes**

1 teaspoon **coriander seeds**

6 **cloves**

6 **green cardamom pods**

2 **onions**, finely diced

3 cloves of **garlic**, crushed

4cm piece of **ginger**, peeled and finely grated

2 tablespoons **tomato purée**

750g **butternut squash**, peeled, deseeded and cut into 2cm chunks

400g **canned cooked chickpeas**, drained

400ml **hot water** (or enough to cover)

250g **kale** or **cavolo nero**, stems removed, leaves finely shredded

freshly squeezed lemon juice, to taste

salt and **freshly ground black pepper**

a handful of **fresh coriander**, to garnish

rice, to serve

We first made this with lamb, but found we love this vegan version more. We also love serving it with Black Rice (see page 169).

Heat the oil in a large, deep pan with a lid, set over a medium heat. Add the mustard seeds and, when they start to pop, reduce the heat and add the cumin, chilli flakes, coriander seeds, cloves, cardamom pods and onions. Cook for about 8 minutes, stirring, until the spices are very fragrant and the onions are soft. Add the garlic, ginger and tomato purée and cook for about 3 minutes, stirring, until the raw smell is cooked out. Add a pinch of salt, the butternut squash, chickpeas and enough hot water to cover. Cover with the lid and gently simmer for 25–35 minutes, until the squash is tender. Remove the lid and stir well, letting the squash break down a little to thicken the sauce.

Add the kale or cavolo nero to the pan, pushing it down to submerge it in the sauce. Increase the heat and simmer for 5 minutes.

Squeeze over a little lemon juice, then taste for salt and pepper. Serve with rice, scattered with a handful of fresh coriander leaves.

= TIP =

In season, pumpkin and gourds are delicious in this – look out for more exciting varieties and colours than the ubiquitous butternut squash.

KUKU PAKA WITH UGALI

2 tablespoons **neutral cooking oil**

4 skin-on **whole chicken legs**, or 8 bone-in, skin-on **thighs** and **drumsticks**

2 **onions**, finely chopped

4 cloves of **garlic**, crushed

3cm piece of **ginger**, peeled and finely grated

3 **hot green chillies** (deseeded or not, to taste), finely chopped

1 tablespoon **tomato purée**

2 teaspoons **ground cumin**

2 teaspoons **ground coriander**

1½ teaspoons **ground turmeric**

2 x 400ml cans **full-fat coconut milk** (cans well-shaken)

1 teaspoon **tamarind paste** or **concentrate** (or add **freshly squeezed lemon juice** at the end of cooking)

salt and **freshly ground black pepper**

a handful of **fresh coriander**, to garnish

This is a Kenyan-style chicken curry, where roasting the meat beforehand results in deliciously crispy skin. When Rebecca first tried it, working in Kenya in 2007, she ate it with ugali – a thick, creamy cornmeal. (She also went skinny-dipping for the first and only time, but that's another story!)

Heat the oven to 190°C/375°F/gas mark 5.

Pour 1 tablespoon of the oil into a roasting pan (in which all the chicken can fit in a single snug layer), then add the chicken. Roast for 40 minutes, basting once with the juices, halfway through.

Meanwhile, make the sauce. Add the other tablespoon of oil to a saucepan set over a medium heat. When hot, add the onions and cook for about 8 minutes, until softened and just starting to brown. Add the garlic, ginger and green chillies and cook for 2–3 minutes, until fragrant, then add the tomato purée. Cook, stirring, for 2 minutes, then add the ground spices and cook for 1 minute, just to toast them briefly. Pour in the coconut milk and add the tamarind, if using. Stir well and remove from the heat. If the chicken still has longer to cook, set the sauce aside.

To make the ugali, pour the water into a large, high-sided saucepan and bring back to the boil. Pour in the cornmeal/polenta in a steady stream, stirring quickly, to prevent lumps forming. Cook, stirring all the time, until smooth and very thick. Taste – it will be very bland and shouldn't be gritty. Continue to cook, still stirring often, until the mixture is thick enough to pull away from the sides of the pan, about 15 minutes. Set aside, off the heat, to firm up for a few minutes while the chicken finishes cooking.

FOR THE UGALI:
800–900ml **freshly boiled water**
250g **coarse white** (or **yellow**) **cornmeal/polenta** (not 'quick-cook')

FOR THE GREENS:
400g **kale**, **spring greens**, **large leaf spinach** or **chard**, tough stems removed, finely shredded and freshly washed
1 **red chilli**, finely diced
salt and **freshly ground black pepper**

Don't cook the ugali too far in advance, as it will set. (Traditionally, no salt or pepper is added to ugali, but feel free to, if you prefer.)

Remove the roasted chicken from the oven. Spoon off any excess fat, if there is a lot in the pan, but leave the cooking juices behind. Pour the curry sauce over the chicken, spooning some sauce over each piece. Arrange so that the chicken pieces are all sitting skin-side up with the skin out of the sauce, and return to the oven for a final 10 minutes to crisp up.

Meanwhile, set a large frying pan over a high heat and add a splash of oil. When hot, add the wet greens and the chilli. Sauté until wilted, then remove from the heat and drain (if necessary). Keep warm until ready to serve.

Use two large serving spoons to shape the ugali into firm, neat oblongs, about the size and shape of a small baked potato. Serve these and the greens alongside the chicken, with the curry sauce spooned over the meat. Finish with a squeeze of lemon, if you didn't use tamarind, and garnish with a handful of coriander leaves.

≡ TIP ≡

For more richly flavoured greens, sauté 1 diced onion, 1 crushed clove of garlic and 1 teaspoon of tomato purée in the pan first, then braise the wet greens, covered with a lid, for 5 minutes or so.

CHICKEN DOPIAZA

SERVES 4

PREP TIME: 15 MINS • COOK TIME: 1¼ HOURS

WF • GF • DF (if substituting the yoghurt) • NF • SoF (check flatbreads) • SUITABLE FOR FREEZING

2 tablespoons **neutral cooking oil**

3 **onions**, 2 finely sliced, 1 cut into
2cm chunks

7 tablespoons **full-fat plain yoghurt**
(substitute non-dairy yoghurt,
if wished)

¼ teaspoon **hot chilli powder**

1 teaspoon **sweet paprika**

1 teaspoon **ground turmeric**

800g bone-in **chicken thighs** and
drumsticks (skin-on or off)

3cm piece of **ginger**, peeled and grated

2 cloves of **garlic**, crushed

½ teaspoon **ground coriander**

¼ teaspoon **ground cinnamon**

½ teaspoon **ground cumin**

6 **green cardamom pods**

400g **canned chopped tomatoes**

2 medium **green chillies**, slit lengthways

freshly squeezed lemon juice

salt and **freshly ground black pepper**

warm flatbreads or **steamed basmati
rice**, to serve

*This is an Afghani dish. The name means 'two onions' – the first lot are
browned and the second simmered and softened in the tangy sauce.*

Heat the oil in a large pan with a lid, set over a medium heat. Add the sliced onions
and cook for 15–20 minutes, stirring often, until dark golden and sticky-looking –
turn the heat to low if they start to char.

Meanwhile, stir together 6 tablespoons of the yoghurt with the chilli powder, paprika
and turmeric, then add the chicken and marinate briefly while the onions cook.

Add the ginger, garlic, coriander, cinnamon, cumin and cardamom pods to the pan
and cook for 1–2 minutes, stirring all the time, until fragrant. Tip the chicken and
marinade into the pan, and cook for about 5 minutes, still stirring, until the onions
and yoghurt have cooked together to form a thick, fragrant, oily-looking paste.

Add the tomatoes and cook for 3–4 minutes, using the tomato juice to deglaze the
pan and scrape up anything that has stuck to the bottom. Pour in 300ml hot water
and add the chillies, plus a little salt and pepper. Bring to a simmer, then reduce the
heat, cover with the lid and cook for 30 minutes.

Remove the lid and add the onion chunks. Increase the heat to allow the extra liquid
to reduce and cook for 15 minutes.

Check the chicken is cooked through and that the onion chunks are beautifully soft.
Remove the pan from the heat and let stand for 5 minutes. Just before serving, stir
through the last tablespoon of yoghurt and a little squeeze of lemon juice. Serve
with flatbreads or rice.

═ TIP ═

As with many curries, you could make this with other meats or fish. If using lamb, just increase the simmering time and make sure there is enough liquid for the extra time. If using fish, don't marinate it in the yoghurt and add to the curry 5 minutes before the end of cooking.

≡ TIP ≡

This freezes well and leftovers can be used to fill pittas or wraps, or even stirred into spiced scrambled eggs or omelettes.

MATT'S LAMB KEEMA WITH WHOLE SPICES, METHI & PEAS

SERVES 4
PREP TIME: 15 MINS • COOK TIME: 55 MINS
WF • GF • NF • SoF

3cm stick of **cinnamon**

3 **green cardamon pods**

7 **black peppercorns**

3 **cloves**

½ teaspoon **cumin seeds**

4 tablespoons **rapeseed oil**, or any neutral **cooking oil**

2 **red onions**, diced

3 cloves of **garlic**, crushed to a paste

3cm piece of **ginger**, peeled and finely grated

750g **minced lamb**

2 teaspoons **ground coriander**

1 teaspoon **ground cumin**

1–1½ teaspoons **chilli powder**

½ teaspoon **ground turmeric**

1 tablespoon **dried fenugreek leaves (methi)**

3 tablespoons **full-fat plain yoghurt**

5 tablespoons **passata**

1½ teaspoons **salt**

250g **frozen peas**

steamed basmati rice and **Dhal** (see pages 26 or 79), to serve

Matt Sefton and his partner Carmel were 'best people' to Steve (who photographed the food in this book), when he married Rebecca (who helped write this book). Years before that, Matt taught Steve how to cook when they lived in a house-share in Brixton – for which Rebecca is forever grateful. This is Matt's recipe for lamb keema, which he likes to serve with a smoky, garlicky dhal and basmati rice.

Dry-fry the whole spices in a wide pan with a lid, set over a high heat. After about 30 seconds, add the oil and the onions and cook for 7–8 minutes, until the onions are turning golden at the edges. Add the garlic and ginger and cook for 1–2 minutes, until fragrant. Push the onion mixture to the side of the pan and add the lamb, breaking it up with a spoon as you go. Cook for about 10 minutes, stirring often, until no traces of pink remain and most of the liquid has evaporated.

Add the ground spices and the fenugreek leaves, and cook for a few moments, then reduce the heat to medium and slowly stir in the yoghurt, then add the passata and the salt.

Reduce the heat to low, cover with the lid and cook for about 25–30 minutes, stirring frequently. Just before the end of cooking, add the frozen peas and cook through. Serve with basmati rice and dhal.

CHICKEN BIRYANI

SERVES 4

PREP TIME: 25 MINS, PLUS 40 MINS–24 HOURS MARINATING • COOK TIME: 1 HOUR 10 MINS

WF • GF • NF • SoF

650g skinless, boneless **chicken thighs**, cut into large chunks

FOR THE CHICKEN MARINADE:

4 heaped tablespoons **full-fat Greek yoghurt**

3cm piece of **ginger**, peeled and finely grated

2 cloves of **garlic**, peeled and finely grated or crushed

½ teaspoon **salt**

½ teaspoon **paprika**

½ teaspoon **hot chilli powder**

1 tablespoon **finely chopped mint leaves**

1 tablespoon **finely chopped fresh coriander**

½ teaspoon **ground coriander**

½ teaspoon **ground cumin**

FOR THE BIRYANI:

200g **basmati rice**

450ml **water**

4 **green cardamom pods**

2 **cloves**

2 tablespoons **neutral cooking oil**

2 **onions**, finely sliced

100ml **milk**

This dish is a real show-stopper. It looks much more complex to prepare than it really is – you just need to get each part ready before layering it together and whacking it in the oven for half an hour.

Mix all the chicken marinade ingredients together, then stir in the chicken. Cover and place in the fridge to marinate for as long as you can – 40 minutes–24 hours.

About 40 minutes before you want to cook, prepare the rice. Rinse the rice several times in running water, then cover with cold water and leave to soak for 20 minutes. Drain.

Set a large pan over a high heat and add the measured water, cardamom pods, cloves and a generous pinch of salt. Bring to the boil, then add the drained rice to the pan. Cook for 7 minutes, until about half-done, then remove from the heat, drain again and set aside. Fish out and discard the whole spices.

Meanwhile, set a large, heavy-based, ovenproof pan with a very well-fitting lid over a medium heat. Add 1 tablespoon of the oil and the onions and cook for 20–30 minutes, stirring often, until the onions are caramelized, deep brown, sticky and soft. Remove from the pan and set aside.

While the rice and onions are cooking, make the masala spice mix, if using. Set a small pan over a medium heat and add the bay leaf, cloves, fennel, cumin, coriander and cardamom seeds. Toast just until the whole spices are fragrant, taking care not to

RECIPE CONTINUES ⟶

a generous pinch of **saffron**

salt, to taste

a handful each of **fresh coriander** and **mint**, roughly torn, plus extra to serve

freshly squeezed lemon juice, to serve

FOR THE BIRYANI MASALA (IF USING – SEE TIP):

1 **bay leaf**

3 **cloves**

¼ teaspoon **fennel seeds**

¼ teaspoon **cumin seeds**

¼ teaspoon **coriander seeds**

seeds from 6 **green cardamom pods**

¼ teaspoon **dried red chilli flakes**

¼ teaspoon **ground mace**

¼ teaspoon **ground cinnamon**

generous dusting of **freshly grated nutmeg**

generous grinding of **black pepper**

burn them. Immediately tip it all into a pestle and mortar or spice grinder and add the chilli flakes, mace, cinnamon, nutmeg and black pepper. Grind to a powder – you may need to remove and discard the tough stem of the bay leaf. Set aside.

Place the ovenproof pan that you used to cook the onions back on a medium heat and add the remaining 1 tablespoon of oil. Add the chicken and its marinade, plus 2 heaped teaspoons of the biryani masala, and cook for 7–8 minutes, stirring and turning each piece of meat once or twice.

Warm the milk and add the saffron, to infuse.

Heat the oven to 180°C/350°F/gas mark 4.

Assemble the biryani by arranging the chicken in a single, even layer in the bottom of its pan. Cover with half of the rice, evenly spread out. Drizzle over half of the infused saffron milk. Sprinkle over half of the coriander and mint and half of the caramelized onions. Repeat. Sprinkle over a pinch of salt, then place a layer of baking paper over the pan and set the lid on top, to form a tight seal. Place in the oven and cook for 30 minutes.

Ideally, take straight to the table and remove the lid there, as it will release a cloud of amazingly fragrant steam. Squeeze over a little lemon juice and garnish with a little extra coriander and mint, just before serving. Eat immediately.

TIP

You can use ready-made biryani masala spice mix – making it fresh gives the richest flavour, but it's easy to track down in supermarkets.

EMILY'S AMAZING BIRMINGHAM BALTI

SERVES 4–6

PREP TIME: 20 MINS • COOK TIME: 2–8 HOURS

NF • SoF (check naan)

3 tablespoons **neutral cooking oil**, plus extra for greasing

1 **whole chicken**, or 6–8 bone-in **thighs** (skin-on or off)

3–4 **onions** (more if you want a less saucy curry), cut into chunks

3 cloves of **garlic**, crushed (or more, to taste)

4cm piece of **ginger**, peeled and diced

1 large **tomato**, finely diced

2 teaspoons **garam masala**

1 teaspoon **ground coriander**

½ teaspoon **chilli powder** (or more, to taste)

a generous pinch of **salt**

1 teaspoon **ground turmeric**

250ml **water**, or more as needed

Naan (see page 198), to serve

a handful of **fresh coriander**, to garnish

Birmingham is famous for baltis – there's no taste like it. A native Brummie, Emily Hawkley is LEON's operations manager: 'I LIVE for a good balti. The longer you can cook it the better. The reason Brummies go for a curry at 2–3am is because it tastes AMAZING late-night, after a few beers. It's cooked in huge pots all evening, then flashed over a hot flame with your order just before serving.'

Heat the oven to 190°C/375°F/gas mark 5. Lightly grease a roasting pan with oil.

Roast the chicken in the oiled pan, basting once or twice, until cooked through (40–50 minutes for thighs; 1–1½ hours for a whole chicken, depending on size). Remove from the oven and let cool. Strip all the meat from the bones and refrigerate until ready to eat.

Meanwhile, heat the oil in a heavy-based pan with a lid over a medium-low heat. Add the onions, garlic and ginger and fry for about 10 minutes, until the onions are soft and translucent, but not browned. Add the remaining ingredients, except the water. Stir and cook for 3–5 minutes, until everything comes together and begins to look saucy and oily. Add the water, bring up to a simmer and cook for 20–25 minutes, stirring every now and then.

RECIPE CONTINUES ⟶

For a quick curry, you can blend the sauce at this point, but ideally cook it slowly, covered with a lid, for several hours, or even all day over a *very* low heat (or in a slow cooker on low for 6–8 hours). Stir often, and add a splash of water if it gets too dry.

When ready to serve, you can leave the sauce as it is, or blend a little, or a lot for a smoother balti sauce. When you're happy, add the torn cooked chicken to the curry.

If you have small metal balti dishes for serving, place them over a high heat and flash the curry in individual portions, to heat and thicken. If not, reheat in the pan and serve in well-warmed bowls, with breads on the side for dipping. Sprinkle with fresh coriander and ENJOY.

≡ TIP ≡

1. Good garam masala is key. Try your local world food store – it's worth the extra pennies.
2. Ideally, eat from a steel dish that you can heat over a flame. If not, make sure your bowl is hot before serving.
3. You can add any protein you like to this instead of the chicken – chickpeas, Curry-Spiced Tofu (see page 102) or pre-cooked meat. Alternatively, cook chunks of fish or prawns directly in the sauce.

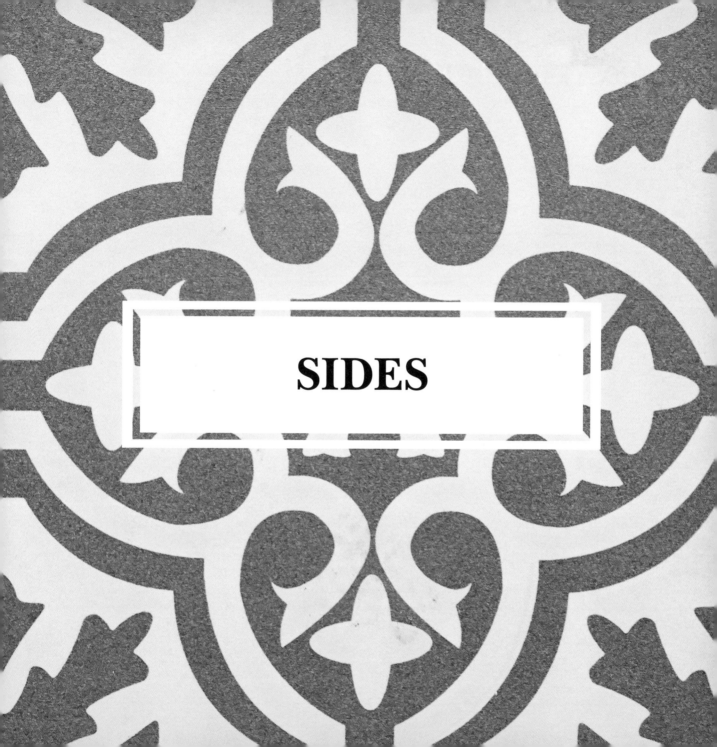

SIDES

ONION BHAJIS

250g **chickpea flour/besan**

1 teaspoon **ground turmeric**

½ teaspoon **garam masala**

¼ teaspoon **asafoetida** or **garlic powder** (optional)

2 tablespoons **roughly chopped fresh coriander**

1 medium **green chilli**, deseeded and finely diced

200–300ml **cold water**

1 tablespoon **vegetable oil**, plus extra for cooking

1 tablespoon **freshly squeezed lime juice** (about ½ lime)

2 **onions**, quartered, then very finely sliced

salt and **freshly ground black pepper**

Chutneys (see pages 215–17), **Raita** (see pages 163–4), and/or **Tamarind Yoghurt** (see page 165), to serve

This recipe makes a LOT of bhajis (also known as onion pakora or pakoda), but they reheat very well; either refrigerate or freeze, then defrost and crisp up in the oven at 200ºC/400ºF/gas mark 6 for 3–4 minutes.

Mix all the dry ingredients together with ½ teaspoon of salt and some black pepper. Add the coriander and green chilli, then whisk in enough water to make a smooth, thick batter. Add the oil and lime juice, then whisk again.

Mix the sliced onions and batter together.

Set a deep, high-sided pan over a high heat and pour in a 6cm depth of cooking oil. Heat to 175°C (if you have a pan thermometer), or until a cube of day-old bread fizzes and browns in 30 seconds.

Carefully add a little bit of the mixture to the pan and cook for 1–2 minutes, until golden. Cool slightly, then taste to check the seasoning.

When happy, use a flat dessertspoon to scoop up 4 or 5 little parcels of the batter and onion and slide gently into the hot oil. They should fizz merrily and then turn golden brown in about 4 minutes – any quicker and the onion won't cook, so turn the heat down as needed. Turn each bhaji in the oil at least once so they cook evenly.

Remove with a slotted spoon to drain further on a plate lined with kitchen paper. Keep warm while you cook the rest. Serve with chutneys, raita and/or tamarind yoghurt.

≡ TIP ≡

Three words for you: onion bhaji sandwiches. Just add chutney and raita.

≡ TIP ≡

Don't skimp on the time this needs
in the food processor – beating the
fish to a paste gives the fishcakes that
bouncy texture you will know from Thai
restaurants.

THAI FISHCAKES

SERVES 4 AS A SIDE OR STARTER (MAKES 8–10 FISHCAKES)
PREP TIME: 20 MINS • COOK TIME: 15 MINS
WF • GF • DF • NF • SoF

250g **white fish** (we like basa)

1 **egg white**

1½ tablespoons **Thai red curry paste** (see page 43, or shop-bought)

a generous pinch of **sugar**

2 teaspoons **fish sauce**, or more to taste

50g **long green beans**, trimmed and finely chopped into 5mm pieces

3 **lime leaves**, stems removed, very finely chopped

neutral cooking oil, for frying

lime wedges, to serve

a handful of **fresh coriander**, to garnish

FOR THE DIPPING SAUCE:

2 tablespoons **ready-made sweet chilli sauce**

2 tablespoons **water**

4 teaspoons **fish sauce**

2 tablespoons **finely chopped cucumber**

1 tablespoon **very finely chopped roasted peanuts**

1 teaspoon very finely chopped **shallot**

We sort of wish we hadn't discovered how easy these are to make. Because now we can't stop.

Place the fish, egg white, curry paste, sugar and fish sauce into a food processor and blitz for 4–5 minutes (depending on the power of your food processor), scraping down the sides a few times as needed, until completely smooth. You should have a pale pink purée with a fairly sticky texture. Stir in the green beans and lime leaves and mix thoroughly.

Mix together the dipping sauce ingredients and set aside.

Pour a 1cm depth of cooking oil into a frying pan with fairly high sides. Heat until shimmering hot (about 175°C if you have a pan thermometer).

Drop a nugget of the fishcake mixture into the hot oil and fry for about 1 minute, until golden and cooked through. Taste and decide whether the mixture needs more fish sauce. When happy with the flavour, shape the fishcakes into 5cm round patties, using your hands (this is quite messy as the mix is sticky, so you can use two large spoons to shape, if you prefer).

Slide the patties into the hot oil and fry for about 2 minutes on each side, turning with a heat-proof spatula, until a deep, golden brown. (Don't crowd the pan as the oil will cool down and the patties will cook too slowly and be greasy.) Remove from the oil with tongs, letting the excess oil drain back into the pan, and set to drain on a plate lined with kitchen paper while you cook the rest.

Serve with the dipping sauce and lime wedges, with coriander leaves to garnish.

ALOO TIKKI

MAKES ABOUT 20

PREP TIME: 20 MINS, PLUS 1 HOUR CHILLING • COOK TIME: 35 MINS

WF • GF (if using gluten-free flour) • V • Ve (if using oil or vegan ghee) • NF • SoF • SUITABLE FOR FREEZING

plain flour, for coating

salt and freshly ground black pepper

neutral cooking oil or ghee, for frying

FOR THE ALOO TIKKI MIXTURE:

1kg floury potatoes, unpeeled, cut into
large chunks

1 tablespoon neutral cooking oil

1 teaspoon black mustard seeds

1 large onion, very finely diced

3 cloves of garlic, crushed

5cm piece of ginger, peeled and finely
grated

1 hot green chilli (deseeded or not, to
taste), very finely chopped

½ teaspoon ground turmeric

1 teaspoon ground cumin

1 teaspoon ground coriander

2 tablespoons freshly squeezed lemon
juice (½ lemon), or more to taste

3 tablespoons very finely chopped fresh
coriander

2 tablespoons plain flour

salt and freshly ground black pepper

Raita (see pages 163–4) or Coriander or
Tamarind Chutney (see pages 215 and
217), to serve

Delicately spiced potato cakes – excellent as a side dish and perfect for parties. Try adding defrosted frozen peas to the mix too.

Cook the potatoes in boiling salted water for about 10 minutes, until only just tender. Drain and spread out in a colander to steam dry; this will ensure your patties are firm not squashy. When cool enough to handle, chop into smaller pieces, then place in a bowl and roughly mash – it doesn't need to be smooth (we keep the skins in the mix).

Heat the oil in a small frying pan over a medium heat. Add the mustard seeds and, when they start to crackle, add the onion and a pinch of salt. Cook for about 8 minutes, stirring, until the onion begins to brown. Reduce the heat, add the garlic, ginger, chilli and ground spices and cook for 2 minutes, stirring. Stir this mixture into the potatoes, along with the lemon juice, coriander, flour and some black pepper. Taste and add more salt or lemon juice, if needed – it should be very well seasoned.

Chill the mixture in the fridge for 1 hour (or in the freezer for 20 minutes).

Pour a layer of flour onto a plate and season well. Pour a 5mm depth of oil or ghee (or a mixture) into a large frying pan and set over a high heat until shimmering hot.

Roll pieces of mash to the size of ping pong balls, then roll them in the flour and gently squash flat with your palm, until about 4cm wide and 2cm thick. Dust off excess flour and carefully slide the patties into the hot oil. Cook for about 2 minutes on each side, until golden and crisp on the bottoms, then flip and repeat. Remove to drain on kitchen paper and keep warm while you cook the rest.

Serve hot, with raita or coriander or tamarind chutney.

PEA & POTATO SAMOSAS

MAKES 16

PREP TIME: 35 MINS • COOK TIME: 50 MINS

DF • V • VE • NF • SoF • SUITABLE FOR FREEZING

neutral cooking oil, for frying

Coconut Chutney (see page 217) and

   Tamarind Yoghurt (see page 165),

   to serve

FOR THE PASTRY:

175g **plain flour**, plus extra for dusting

¼ teaspoon **salt**

1½ tablespoons **neutral cooking oil**

FOR THE FILLING:

450g **white potato**, peeled and diced

200g (1 large) **carrot**, peeled and diced

1 tablespoon **neutral cooking oil**, plus

   extra as needed

1 **onion**, finely diced

2 cloves of **garlic**, grated

4cm piece of **ginger**, peeled and grated

½ teaspoon **ground turmeric**

½ teaspoon **dried red chilli flakes**

   (optional)

1 teaspoon **garam masala**

1 teaspoon **mustard seeds**

75g **frozen peas**

2 tablespoons **finely chopped fresh**

   coriander

We developed this version of the classic samosa for our book, **Fast Vegan.** *We like it so much we decided to include it here, too.*

First, make the pastry. Combine the flour and salt in a bowl, then rub in the oil with your fingers. When the mixture is sandy, add enough water (50–60ml) to form a dough. You may not need it all, as the dough should not be sticky. When the dough is still quite dry and craggy, knead for up to 5 minutes, until smooth and elastic. Place the ball of dough into a clean bowl, cover with clingfilm or a tea towel, and set aside to rest while you make the filling.

Cook the potato and carrot in a large pan of salted boiling water for about 15 minutes, until tender.

Meanwhile, heat the oil in a frying pan over a medium heat. When hot, add the onion and a pinch of salt and sauté for about 8 minutes, until translucent and beginning to brown. Add the garlic and ginger and cook, stirring, for 1 minute. Add the turmeric, chilli flakes, if using, garam masala and mustard seeds, plus another splash of oil if the pan seems dry. Cook for 1 minute, then remove from the heat. Add the frozen peas and coriander leaves, stir and set aside.

Drain the potato and carrot, then roughly mash, leaving some chunks for texture. Stir in the contents of the onion pan, along with the lemon juice and some black pepper. Taste and add more salt, if needed.

RECIPE CONTINUES ➡

1 teaspoon **lemon juice**
salt and **freshly ground black pepper**

Set a deep, high-sided pan over a medium heat and pour in a 4cm depth of cooking oil. Heat to 175°C (if you have a pan thermometer), or until a cube of day-old bread fizzes and browns in 30 seconds.

Meanwhile, divide the pastry dough into 8 pieces, then shape into neat balls. Dust a work surface and rolling pin with flour, then roll out one ball to a very thin circle of pastry, about 20cm across. Use a sharp knife to halve the circle. Shape the semi-circle of pastry into a cone by folding it over on itself, one third at a time. Wet the outer edge of the pastry and thoroughly seal it like a seam, pinching it firmly shut at the bottom of the cone so that the filling doesn't leak when frying.

To fill, make a ring with your thumb and forefinger and use it to support the open-topped cone. Use a spoon to fill the cone about three-quarters full, then wet the remaining open edges and pinch firmly shut.

Repeat until all the pastry is used up.

Fry 2 or 3 samosas at a time, for 2–3 minutes on each side, until golden brown and bubbly all over. Use a slotted spoon or tongs to remove them from the pan, draining any excess oil back into the pan. Set to drain on a plate lined with kitchen paper and keep warm while you cook the rest.

Serve hot, with coconut chutney and tamarind yoghurt, plus some Indian pickles.

≡ TIP ≡

To reheat, defrost if frozen, then place in the oven at 200°C/400°F/gas mark 6 for 8–10 minutes.

RAITA

2 teaspoons **neutral cooking oil**

½ teaspoon **black mustard seeds**

75g (approx. 12cm piece) **cucumber**, deseeded and finely diced

75g (1 small) **carrot**, very finely diced (optional)

8 heaped tablespoons **thick full-fat plain yoghurt** (can be non-dairy)

leaves from 1 bushy sprig of **mint**, finely chopped

a pinch of **sea salt**, or to taste

a small pinch of **sugar** (optional)

We have included twelve different kinds of raita in this book. We're obsessed.

Heat the oil in a small pan set over a medium heat. When hot, add the mustard seeds and as soon as they start to pop, remove from the heat.

Place the cucumber, carrot (if using), yoghurt, mint leaves, salt and mustards seeds (leaving most of the oil behind) in a bowl. Mix, then taste and decide if you want to add sugar or more salt.

Set aside until ready to serve. This will keep for 1–2 days, covered, in the fridge.

≡ TIP ≡

There are so many variations! Add finely diced shallot; ground cumin, toasted briefly after cooking the mustard seeds; 4–5 cherry tomatoes, deseeded and very finely chopped; a good pinch of chilli powder; chaat masala spice mix; or leftover cooked vegetables, finely chopped, such as aubergine, okra, green beans, cabbage or cauliflower. Yum.

RINKU'S POMEGRANATE & CORIANDER RAITA

SERVES 4 AS A SIDE
PREP TIME: 15 MINS, PLUS 1 HOUR CHILLING • COOK TIME: 1 MIN
WF • GF • DF • V • Ve (if substituting the yoghurt) **• NF • SoF** (unless using nut or soy yoghurt)

1 tablespoon **cumin seeds**

1 large **pomegranate**

400ml **full-fat plain yoghurt** (can be non-dairy) or **full-fat Greek yoghurt**

a handful of **fresh coriander,** finely chopped

a handful of **fresh mint,** finely chopped

1 teaspoon **black salt** (or a generous pinch of **sea salt**, if preferred)

2 tablespoons **freshly squeezed lime juice**

1 tablespoon **brown sugar**

¼ teaspoon **freshly ground black pepper**

¼ teaspoon **chilli powder** (optional)

== TIP ==

Any leftover pomegranate seeds will make a lovely garnish for almost any curry in this book – at LEON, we use them in wraps and over mezze-style salads. They are rich in antioxidants and release a juicy burst of tanginess when you pop them in your mouth.

A crunchy and cooling side for spicy mains (or barbecued meats or grilled fish). If you love the sauce in the LEON lamb kofte wrap, you will love this – try it with the Lamb Keema on page 145.

Place a small frying pan over a medium heat. Dry-roast the cumin seeds until fragrant, taking care not to burn them. Remove from the heat and allow to cool, then grind to a fine powder.

Cut the pomegranate in half and tap the top gently with a tablespoon over a bowl – the seeds should gently loosen and fall out. Take the remaining seeds out by hand, ensuring no white pith comes with them.

Mix all of the ingredients in a large bowl, reserving about 1 tablespoon of pomegranate seeds and a good pinch of the chopped coriander leaves, for garnish. Cover and place the bowl in the fridge for at least 1 hour, to allow the flavours to develop.

Take the raita out of the fridge 30 minutes before serving, to allow it to reach room temperature. Give it a final stir and garnish with the reserved pomegranate seeds and coriander.

TAMARIND YOGHURT

SERVES 4
PREP TIME: 5 MINS
WF • GF • V • DF • Ve (if substituting the yoghurt) **• NF • SoF** (unless using nut or soy yoghurt)

2 teaspoons **tamarind paste** or
   concentrate
125ml **full-fat plain yoghurt** (can be
non-dairy)
2 teaspoons **finely chopped fresh mint**
a pinch of **ground cumin**
a pinch of **salt**

For dipping, drizzling and dolloping.

Stir all the ingredients together, then taste and add more salt, as needed.

RINKU'S BEETROOT PACHADI

SERVES 4 AS A SIDE
PREP TIME: 8 MINS • COOK TIME: 2 MINS
WF • GF • DF • V • Ve (if substituting the yoghurt) • NF • SoF (unless using nut or soy yoghurt)

3 medium **pre-cooked beetroot** (not in vinegar), chopped into 2cm chunks

200ml **full-fat plain yoghurt** (can be non-dairy)

25g **desiccated coconut**

2 **green chillies** (deseeded or not, to taste)

2cm piece of **ginger**, peeled and finely grated

salt, to taste

water, as required

1 tablespoon **rapeseed oil**

1 teaspoon **black mustard seeds**

1 tablespoon **curry leaves**

≡ TIP ≡

If cooking the beetroot yourself from scratch, wash, then wrap each one in foil. Roast for about 45 minutes at 180°C/350°F/gas mark 4, or until tender to the point of a knife. Cool, then rub off the skins with your thumbs.

Rebecca would like to thank her friend Rinku for patiently teaching her all sorts of curry lore and wisdom. And for feeding her. 'Pachadi is from Kerala and Tamil Nadu. The base is coconut and yoghurt, and seasonal vegetables are then added. In our home, it is very popular, I think because of the gorgeous colour.'

Place the beetroot, yoghurt, coconut, chillies, ginger and a pinch of salt into a blender or food processor. Add very little water to begin with and briefly blitz, adding more water as necessary to help it come together. We like to have a few bits of beetroot that haven't been completely blended in, so usually two 15-second blitzes will do the trick. Taste for salt and add as needed. Transfer the mixture to a nice serving bowl.

Heat the oil in a small saucepan over a medium heat. When hot, add the black mustard seeds and the curry leaves and cook for 15 seconds, or until the curry leaves are aromatic. Remove from the heat, pour this temper over the pachadi mixture and serve.

RICE

COCONUT RICE

SERVES 4
PREP TIME: 5 MINS • COOK TIME: 11
MINS, PLUS 10 MINS STANDING
WF • GF • DF • V • Ve • NF • SoF

250g **uncooked jasmine rice**
275ml **full-fat coconut milk** (from a well-shaken can)
a pinch of **salt**

This rice is excellent with fiercely spicy dishes, and most South Asian curries. Low-fat coconut milk is liable to split, so make sure you use a good-quality full-fat type.

Rinse the rice well under cold running water. Tip into a pan with a lid, then mix in 250ml water, the coconut milk and salt. Bring to the boil, then reduce the heat, cover and simmer for 11 minutes.

Remove from the heat, take the lid off and fluff up the grains of rice with a fork. Replace the lid and leave to steam for 10 minutes, then serve.

CURD RICE

SERVES 4
PREP TIME: 10 MINS • COOK TIME: 2 MINS
WF • GF • V • DF • NF • SoF

700g **freshly cooked basmati rice** (or 250g **uncooked rice**, steamed)
1 tablespoon **neutral cooking oil**
½ teaspoon each **mustard** and **cumin seeds**
5 **curry leaves**, torn into little pieces
1 **green chilli**, deseeded and finely chopped (optional)
½ teaspoon **asafoetida**
4 heaped tablespoons **full-fat plain yoghurt**
a handful of **fresh coriander**, to garnish
2 tablespoons **pomegranate seeds**, to serve

A soothing mellow rice, made with yoghurt.

Set the freshly cooked rice aside to cool to warm, as very hot rice may make the yoghurt split.

Heat the oil in a small frying pan set over a medium heat. Add the mustard seeds and, when they start to pop, add the cumin seeds, curry leaves and chilli, if using. Sizzle for 1 minute, then remove from the heat and add the asafoetida.

Spoon the yoghurt into the warm rice and mix well, then add the tempered spices and the oil from the pan. Mix well and serve immediately, topped with the coriander leaves and pomegranate seeds (or chill completely, immediately, and eat cold – but do not keep for more than 24 hours).

BLACK RICE

SERVES 4
PREP TIME: 1 MIN • COOK TIME: 45–50
MINS, PLUS 10 MINS STANDING
WF • GF • DF • V • Ve • NF • SoF

250g **black/forbidden rice**
1.2 litres **water**
a generous pinch of **salt**

TIP

If you can't find black rice, look out for red
rice, or mixed basmati and wild rice, as a
change from white rice.

Nutty and with lots of bite, black rice is a very nutritious alternative to the white stuff. (We are also fans of brown rice at LEON and we've a lot of time for quinoa, too.) Whether or not to rinse and soak black rice is up for debate – some reckon doing both means that good antioxidants are lost, while others say it cooks more quickly and is less sticky if you do. What isn't in question, though, is that those anthocyanins that make it so good for us will stain anything they can – clothes, ceramic or enamel pans and worktops – so be careful.

Place everything in a pan with a well-fitting lid and bring up to a simmer over a medium heat. Reduce the heat to low, cover and cook for 45–50 minutes, stirring once or twice so it doesn't stick to the bottom of the pan, until the rice is tender but with a little bite.

Remove from the heat, fluff the rice grains up with a fork, then cover again and leave to stand for 10 minutes or so, before serving.

JEERA RICE

SERVES 4
PREP TIME: 5 MINS, PLUS 30 MINS SOAKING
COOK TIME: 14 MINS, PLUS 10 MINS
STANDING
WF • GF • DF • V • Ve • NF • SoF

250g **basmati rice**
2 tablespoons **neutral cooking oil**
1 teaspoon **cumin seeds**
a pinch of **salt**

Fragrant, earthy rice flavoured with cumin seeds (aka jeera).

Rinse the rice well under cold running water. Place in a bowl, cover with cold water and leave to soak for up to 30 minutes. Drain.

Heat the oil in a large saucepan with a lid, set over a medium heat. When hot, add the cumin seeds and toast for 30 seconds. Add the rice and toss for 1–2 minutes, letting the oil coat the grains of rice. Add 500ml water and the salt, cover and bring to the boil. Reduce the heat to low and simmer for 12 minutes.

Remove the lid, fluff up the grains of rice with a fork, then replace the lid and leave to steam for a further 5–10 minutes.

5 WAYS WITH CAULIFLOWER RICE

SERVES 4
PREP TIME: 5 MINS • COOK TIME: 7 MINS, PLUS 3–4 MINS STANDING
WF • GF • DF • V • VE • NF • SoF

600g **cauliflower florets**
2 teaspoons **neutral cooking oil**
salt

≡ VARIATIONS ≡

FOR SOUTH ASIAN OR JAPANESE DISHES: cook as here, then add a splash of **soy sauce**, a handful of chopped **spring onions** and ½ teaspoon peeled and finely grated **ginger** or a dash of **sesame oil**. Mix very well before serving.

FOR THAI DISHES: cook as here, then dress to taste with a little **fish sauce** and freshly squeezed **lime juice**, off the heat. (Add ½ teaspoon of each to begin with.)

FOR INDIAN DISHES: before cooking the cauliflower, and in the same pan and oil, toast a pinch of **mustard seeds** until they pop, then add a pinch of **cumin seeds**, 1 crushed clove of **garlic** and ¼ teaspoon **ground turmeric**. Cook for 1 minute, before adding the **cauliflower**, then cook as here.

FOR COCONUT STICKY 'RICE': cook as here, then dress with 1–2 tablespoons **coconut milk** and a pinch of **salt**.

A low-carb substitute for traditional rice, we were happily surprised by how well this works when we first tried making it.

Place some of the cauliflower florets into the bowl of a food processor, filling it no more than halfway. Whizz for 15–20 seconds – you want grains about the size of small couscous, but no finer, or the 'rice' will be mushy when cooked. If larger pieces remain, tip everything into a bowl, pick out the big bits and process them on their own. Repeat until all the cauliflower is couscous-like.

To cook, use the widest frying pan you have, so that the cauliflower cooks in the thinnest possible layer. Set the pan over a medium-low heat and add the oil, then tip the cauliflower into the pan and spread out in a thin, even layer. Let it cook for 1–2 minutes, then use a heatproof spatula to shimmy it around the pan, then rearrange in a thin layer again. Repeat this process 3 times, letting the cauliflower become golden in places.

Remove from the heat, stir and leave in the hot pan for 3–4 minutes, so that even more moisture can evaporate. Serve as it is, seasoned with a little salt, as needed.

≡ TIP ≡

The outer leaves and stem of the cauliflower can be saved and added to slaw, finely sliced. Cool any leftover cauliflower rice and refrigerate immediately, then use within 24 hours in place of couscous in salads.

3 WAYS WITH FRIED RICE

EGG-FRIED RICE WITH SOY SAUCE

SERVES 2 AS A MAIN OR 4 AS A SIDE

PREP TIME: 10 MINS • COOK TIME: 8 MINS

WF • GF (check tamari/soy sauce ingredients) • DF • V • Ve (without egg)

1 tablespoon **neutral cooking oil**

2 cloves of **garlic**, finely sliced (optional)

1 **spring onion**, white and green parts divided, finely diced

350g **cooked short grain Japanese rice** or **jasmine rice** (or 125g **uncooked rice**, cooked)

1 tablespoon **tamari/soy sauce**

1 **egg**, lightly beaten (optional, but recommended)

lime wedges, to serve

This is Japanese-style fried rice, but you can also serve it with Chinese-style recipes. It's a great way to use up leftovers and is soothing – great for colds, flu or hangovers. (Not that we ever have those. Not us.)

Heat the oil in a large frying pan or wok set over a medium-high heat. When hot, add the garlic and white parts of the spring onion and cook for 2 minutes, stirring, until the garlic begins to brown. Add the rice and sprinkle over the tamari/soy sauce, tossing so that it coats the rice evenly, and breaking up any lumps. After 2 minutes, push the rice to the side and add the egg to the pan, if using. Allow it to cook for about 1 minute, moving it around so that it scrambles lightly, then stir it into the rice.

Remove from the heat and serve immediately, sprinkled with the remaining spring onion greens.

= TIP =

Finish with a pinch of sesame seeds, if you fancy.

INDIAN-STYLE FRIED RICE

SERVES 2 AS A MAIN OR 4 AS A SIDE
PREP TIME: 15 MINS • COOK TIME: 8 MINS
WF • GF • DF • V • VE • NF • SoF

1 tablespoon **neutral cooking oil**

½ teaspoon **mustard seeds**

4–5 **curry leaves**

½ teaspoon **cumin seeds**

2 **spring onions**, finely chopped

1–2 cloves of **garlic**, crushed, to taste,

2cm piece of **ginger**, peeled and finely
grated

½ teaspoon **ground turmeric**

350g **cooked leftover basmati rice** (or
125g **uncooked rice**, cooked)

a handful of **fresh coriander leaves**,
chopped

freshly squeezed lemon juice

salt and **freshly ground black pepper**

Rice with tempered seeds and fresh herbs – wonderful on its own or with leftover curry.

Heat the oil in a large pan or wok set over a medium heat. When hot, add the mustard seeds and, when they start to pop, add the curry leaves and cumin seeds. When the cumin is fragrant, add the spring onions, garlic and ginger, and stir-fry for 1 minute or so. Add the turmeric and then the rice and stir-fry until the rice is piping hot and bright yellow throughout.

Remove from the heat and add the coriander leaves, a splash of lemon juice and plenty of salt and pepper. Toss well again, then serve immediately.

TIP

Be sure to chill your leftover rice immediately, and store for no more than 24 hours, otherwise it can be home to some pretty nasty bugs.

THAI-STYLE FRIED RICE

SERVES 2 AS A MAIN OR 4 AS A SIDE
PREP TIME: 10 MINS • COOK TIME: 6 MINS
WF • GF • DF • V • VE (if substituting fish sauce and nam prik pao) • SoF

1 tablespoon **neutral cooking oil**

1 clove of **garlic**, crushed

3 tablespoons chopped **unroasted peanuts** or **cashews** (optional)

2 **spring onions**, finely sliced

1 **hot red chilli** (deseeded or not, to taste), finely chopped

350g **cooked leftover jasmine rice** (or 125g **uncooked rice**, cooked)

2 teaspoons **fish sauce**, plus extra as needed (vegetarians and vegans can omit and add **salt** instead, or a pinch of **seaweed powder**)

200g **Asian greens**, shredded

freshly squeezed lime juice

Sriracha hot sauce or **nam prik pao**, or similar **Thai** or **Asian chilli paste/oil**, to serve

TIP

Add in and stir-fry some seafood, leftover cooked pork or chicken, or egg (or add a fried egg to serve). Finish with Thai basil or fresh coriander.

This was a new discovery for us. And it's one we're so happy to have made.

Heat the oil in a large frying pan or wok set over a medium-high heat. When hot, add the garlic, nuts, if using, spring onions and chilli and sizzle for 1 minute. Add the rice, fish sauce and greens and stir-fry for 3–4 minutes, until the greens are just wilted.

Remove from the heat and squeeze over the lime juice. Drizzle with Sriracha or chilli paste/oil, then toss and taste. Serve immediately.

TIP

Pilau can be made plain by omitting the meat or vegetarian/vegan by swapping the meat for mixed vegetables (fresh or frozen diced carrot, sweetcorn and green beans work well); in which case, omit the 50–60 minutes stove-top cooking in the first step.

SHUMAIYA'S AKHNI PILAU

SERVES 8–10
PREP TIME: 20 MINS • COOK TIME: 1 HOUR 50 MINS
WF • GF • DF (if using oil or non-dairy ghee) **• NF • SoF**

3–4 tablespoons **neutral cooking oil** or **ghee**

3 **onions**, finely chopped

6cm piece of **ginger**, peeled and finely grated

4 cloves of **garlic**, crushed

1 teaspoon **cumin seeds**

6cm stick of **cinnamon**, broken into large pieces

3 **bay leaves**

4 **green cardamom pods**

1kg **beef** or **lamb**, ideally bone-in, cut into 3–4cm chunks

2 teaspoons **salt**

4–5 **green bird's-eye chillies**, sliced lengthways (or less, or omit, to taste)

1 teaspoon **ground coriander**

1½ teaspoons **garam masala**

600ml **hot water** (1½ times the volume of rice)

400g **uncooked basmati rice**

½ teaspoon **ground cinnamon**

finely sliced **hot red** or **green chillies**, to serve (optional)

Our friend Shumi is from a Bengali family. 'This meat pilau is usually served up for special occasions or when guests come to visit. It's made with aromatic spices, so the rice doesn't clash with whatever curry it's being served with.' Serve with a lamb, beef, chicken or vegetable curry, with an onion salad on the side (try the Kachumber Salad on page 192).

Heat enough oil or ghee to cover the base of a large heavy-based pan with a lid, set over a medium heat. Add half each of the onions, ginger and garlic, and cook until golden. Add the cumin seeds, cinnamon, bay leaves, cardamom pods, meat and salt. Stir to combine, then reduce the heat, cover and let the meat stew in its own juices for 50–60 minutes, ensuring it doesn't dry up. Add a dash or two of water, if needed, and stir every 5–10 minutes. Heat the oven to 160°C/325°F/gas mark 3.

When the meat is tender, set a separate large ovenproof pan with a lid over a low-medium heat and add the remaining ghee and onions. Cook for about 8 minutes, until the onions start to soften, then add the remaining ginger and garlic, along with the bird's-eye chillies. Cook for 5 minutes, stirring occasionally. Add the ground coriander and 1 teaspoon of the garam masala and cook for another 5 minutes, until the oil separates from the onions.

Add the cooked meat mixture to the ovenproof pan, along with its juices, and bring to the boil. Pour in the hot water, then add the rice, ground cinnamon and remaining garam masala and stir everything together. Cover and bake in the oven for 25–30 minutes, until all the liquid has been absorbed and the surface looks slightly dry.

Remove from the oven and let stand, with the lid on, for 5 minutes. Serve immediately, garnished with chillies.

COCONUT RICE 'N' PEAS

SERVES 4
PREP TIME: 15 MINS • COOK TIME: 12 MINS, PLUS 8 MINS STANDING
WF • GF • DF • V • VE • NF • SoF

250g **uncooked basmati rice**

250ml **full-fat coconut milk**

400g **canned kidney beans**, **black beans** or **gungo peas** (or a can containing a mix of all 3 beans), drain and reserve the water (see below)

250ml **water** (use the water from the beans can, topped up with more water if needed)

1 **spring onion**, finely chopped

1 medium **red chilli**, slit down one side

1 sprig **fresh thyme** or a tiny pinch of **dried thyme**

salt (optional) and **freshly ground black pepper**

Serve this with the Heartbreak Curry (see page 38), or any Caribbean-style curry.

Wash the rice under cold running water and set aside.

In a large pan with a lid, mix together the coconut milk, beans, measured bean water/water, spring onion, chilli, thyme, a pinch of salt (unless the bean water was already salted) and some black pepper. Bring up to a simmer, then add the washed rice. Cover and cook for 12 minutes, stirring once or twice towards the end of cooking.

Remove from the heat and leave to stand, still covered with a lid, for 5–8 minutes. Fluff up with a fork before serving.

= TIP =

Some recipes recommend using a whole Scotch bonnet, rather than an ordinary chilli – this makes the rice very spicy, but go for it, if you're brave.

CRISPY ONIONS

SERVES 4 AS A TOPPING
PREP TIME: 5 MINS • COOK TIME: 30–35 MINS
WF • GF • DF • V • VE • NF • SoF

3 tablespoons **neutral cooking oil**
2 **onions**, finely sliced into half moons
a pinch of **salt**

There's almost no curry that won't benefit from a handful of crispy onions, especially lentil curries and anything vegan. Take your time over this one – rushing equals burnt and bitter onions. (P.S. You can buy these ready made...)

Heat the oil in a wide frying pan set over the lowest heat possible. Add the onions and cook really slowly for up to 35 minutes, stirring often, until deep brown, nutty, sweet and really crisp.

Lift out with a slotted spoon and drain off any excess oil on kitchen paper. Toss with a little pinch of salt before using.

═ TIP ═
Once cooled, these will keep in a sealed container for 4–5 days. Crisp up in a hot pan before using, if necessary.

STEAMED GREENS

SERVES 4
PREP TIME: 10 MINS • COOK TIME: 10 MINS
DF • WF • GF (check soy sauce ingredients, if using) • V • Ve (if substituting fish sauce) • NF

a splash of **neutral cooking oil**

500g **shredded pak choi** or other **mild Asian greens**, or **tenderstem** or **purple-sprouting broccoli**, **long green beans**, **mangetout**, **sugar-snap peas**, freshly washed and still wet

FOR THAI/VIETNAMESE STYLE:

a pinch of **salt**

1 clove of **garlic**, peeled and bruised

1 tablespoon **fish sauce** (vegetarians/vegans can substitute **soy sauce**)

1 tablespoon **freshly squeezed lime juice** (omit if using soy sauce)

a pinch of **black** or **white sesame seeds**

FOR INDIAN-STYLE:

½ **onion**, chopped

1 clove of **garlic**, crushed

1 teaspoon peeled and finely grated **ginger**

½ teaspoon **cumin seeds**

½ teaspoon **mustard seeds**

½ **green chilli**, finely chopped

1 tablespoon **dessicated coconut** (optional)

salt and **freshly ground black pepper**

freshly squeezed lemon juice, to serve

Greens are at the heart of what we do at LEON (our New Original Salad has been a bestseller for 15 years now), and we know that – done right – they can be so good that nobody will need nudging to eat them. Tweak the seasonings, as below, and these sautéed greens will go with either Indian-style or Southeast Asian-style curries.

FOR THAI/VIETNAMESE-STYLE GREENS:

Heat the oil in a large pan with a lid, set over a medium heat. Add the wet greens or vegetables, salt and garlic (plus a couple of extra tablespoons of water, if the pan seems dry). Cover with a lid and steam for 3–4 minutes, then remove the lid and stir everything a couple of times. If the vegetables need a little more cooking, return the lid to the pan and cook for 1–2 minutes longer, otherwise remove from the heat. Mix together the fish sauce and lime juice (or just use soy sauce) and dress the cooked greens. Sprinkle with black or white sesame seeds before serving.

FOR INDIAN-STYLE GREENS:

Heat the oil in a large pan, set over a medium heat. Add the onion and sauté for 5 minutes, then add the garlic, ginger, cumin seeds, mustard seeds and green chilli. (If serving with something coconutty, add the desiccated coconut at the same time as the spices.) Cook for 5 minutes, until the mustard seeds crackle, then add the greens or vegetables, along with a pinch of salt and pepper. Sauté until the greens are just wilted, or the vegetables are tender, less than 5 minutes. Squeeze over a little lemon juice before serving.

=≡ TIP ≡=

Use the method for Indian-style greens as a way of using up leftover cooked vegetables (or frozen vegetables from a bag), such as carrots, aubergines, potatoes, peas, sweetcorn, cabbage or even Brussels sprouts.

CABBAGE, PEA & POTATO CURRY

SERVES 2 AS A MAIN OR 4 AS A SIDE
PREP TIME: 15 MINS • COOK TIME: 15 MINS
WF • GF • DF • V • Ve • NF • SoF

1 tablespoon **neutral cooking oil**

½ teaspoon **mustard seeds**

¼ teaspoon **cumin seeds**

½ teaspoon **asafoetida**

½ teaspoon **ground turmeric**

4 **curry leaves**

½–1 **green chilli** (deseeded or not, to taste), finely chopped

½ teaspoon **ground coriander**

300g **cabbage**, core and ribs removed, finely shredded

250g **potatoes**, peeled and cut into 1½cm chunks

4 tablespoons **water**

100g **frozen peas**

about 2 teaspoons **freshly squeezed lemon** or **lime juice**, to serve (optional)

salt and **freshly ground black pepper**

=≡ TIP ≡=

Leftovers are great in Curry Wraps (see page 211). This is also good with cauliflower, broken into little florets, either instead of the cabbage or potatoes, or as an extra ingredient.

We love to use sweet green cabbage, such as hispi, here, but any cabbage will work beautifully. If you don't have any asafoetida powder (find it in the spice aisle of the supermarket), use a crushed clove of garlic, or a pinch of onion or garlic powder, instead.

Heat the oil in a large pan with a lid set over a medium heat. Add the mustard seeds and, when they start to crackle, add the cumin seeds. Sizzle for 30 seconds, then quickly add the asafoetida, turmeric, curry leaves, green chilli and coriander. Mix well, letting them cook for no more than 30 seconds, then add the cabbage, potatoes and water, plus a good dose of salt and pepper. Toss well, then reduce the heat to low, cover with the lid and cook for 10 minutes, or until the potatoes are tender.

Add the peas to the pan, mix well again, then cook for a final 2 minutes. (You shouldn't need to, but if there's a lot of liquid, remove the lid and increase the heat to bubble away any excess.) Squeeze over the lemon or lime juice, if using, then taste to check for salt, pepper and lemon levels, adding more as needed.

Serve immediately, as a side dish or as a light main with raita (see pages 163–4) or plain yoghurt, Lime Pickle (see page 214), Mango Chutney (see page 216) and flatbreads, such as roti/chapati (see page 200).

BEETROOT THORAN

SERVES 4 AS A MAIN OR SIDE
PREP TIME: 15 MINS • COOK TIME: 20–27 MINS
WF • GF • DF • V • Ve • NF • SoF

1 tablespoon **neutral cooking oil**

2 teaspoons **mustard seeds**

½ teaspoon **cumin seeds**

75g **shallots**, finely sliced

5 **curry leaves**, torn

½ teaspoon **ground turmeric**

450g **beetroot**, washed, peeled and finely grated (see tip)

3 tablespoons **desiccated coconut**

3 tablespoons **hot water**

salt

This dry, curried vegetable dish from south India can be made with almost any shreddable root vegetable, or you could use shredded cabbage, long green beans, canned unripe green jackfruit or greens, such as spinach.

Heat the oil in a large wide pan with a lid set over a medium heat. When hot, add the mustard seeds and, when they start to crackle and pop, add the cumin seeds and cook for 1–2 minutes, until fragrant. Reduce the heat to low, add the shallots and curry leaves, along with a pinch of salt and cook for 5 minutes, until the shallots have softened a little.

Add the turmeric and then the grated beetroot and desiccated coconut and stir-fry gently for 3–4 minutes. Finally, add the water, cover with a lid and cook gently for 10–15 minutes, stirring once or twice, until the beetroot is tender but still has some bite.

Serve hot, as a side, or with rice or flatbreads (see pages 198–201 and 205–6) and raita (see pages 163–4) as a light lunch.

TIP

Use the grater attachment on a food processor, if you have one, or wear gloves, if you don't want pink fingers.

BOMBAY POTATOES

500g **new** or **baby potatoes**, cut into small chunks

1 tablespoon **neutral cooking oil**

½ teaspoon **mustard seeds**

½ teaspoon **cumin seeds**

1 clove of **garlic**, crushed

2cm piece of **ginger**, peeled and grated

2 teaspoons **tomato purée**

¼ teaspoon **ground turmeric**

salt

freshly squeezed lemon juice, to serve

This is the very easiest version of Bombay potatoes – if you have a little more time, start by softening an onion in the oil, before adding the garlic, ginger and spices.

Simmer the potatoes in a pan of boiling salted water for 12–17 minutes, until tender. Drain.

Towards the end of the potatoes' cooking time, heat the oil in a frying pan over a medium heat. Add the mustard seeds and, when they start to pop, add the cumin seeds, reduce the heat to low and cook for 1 minute. Add the garlic, ginger, tomato purée and turmeric and cook for 2–3 minutes, until fragrant. Add the potatoes to the pan along with 2 tablespoons of water, just enough to loosen the sauce so that it coats the potatoes.

Sauté the potatoes gently, stirring and tossing until hot through and evenly covered in the spiced sauce. Remove from the heat. Sprinkle with a pinch of salt and a squeeze of lemon, stir once again and then serve.

If you have some, frizzle 3 or 4 torn curry leaves in the hot oil, when you add the cumin seeds.

BAKED ALOO GOBI

3 tablespoons **neutral cooking oil**

500g **potatoes**, unpeeled, cut into 2–3cm chunks

2 **onions**, each cut into 6–8 wedges

2 cloves of **garlic**, crushed

3cm piece of **ginger**, peeled and finely grated

¼–½ teaspoon **hot chilli powder**, to taste

½ teaspoon **nigella seeds** (optional)

1 teaspoon **cumin seeds**

1 teaspoon **coriander seeds**

1 teaspoon **tomato purée**

1 small **cauliflower**, chopped into small 2–3cm florets

200g **canned chopped tomatoes** (½ can) or **fresh tomatoes**, chopped

250ml **hot water**

salt and **freshly ground black pepper**

freshly squeezed lemon juice, to serve

a handful of **fresh coriander**, roughly chopped

≡ TIP ≡

Any leftovers? Turn to page 211 and use them in one of our curry wraps.

We do love curries where all you need to do is chuck it all in a tray.

Heat the oven to 190°C/375°F/gas mark 5.

Choose a large, ideally metal, baking dish or roasting tray that will allow all the ingredients to fit in a single layer. Pour in the oil, then add the potatoes and onions. Toss well, then arrange in a single layer. Bake in the oven for 10 minutes.

Remove from the oven and add a dusting of black pepper and a generous pinch of salt, plus the garlic, ginger, chilli powder, nigella seeds, if using, cumin seeds, coriander seeds, tomato purée, cauliflower florets and fresh tomatoes, if using. Toss well, then return to the oven for 20 minutes, stirring once halfway through.

Remove from the oven and mix in the canned tomatoes, if using, and water, then bake for a final 15 minutes, until the potatoes are cooked through and the cauliflower is tender. If it seems watery, don't worry, just give it a good stir to allow the water to incorporate into the tomato-y sauce.

Squeeze over a little lemon juice and stir through half of the coriander. Taste and add more salt, pepper or lemon juice, as needed. Finish with the last of the coriander and serve immediately.

KOSHAMBARI SALAD

150g **yellow mung/moong dal** (also known as **split huskless mung beans**), rinsed

1 tablespoon **neutral cooking oil**

2 teaspoons **mustard seeds**

8 **curry leaves**, roughly torn

2 tablespoons **desiccated coconut**

50g **unroasted peanuts** or **cashews**, pummelled or chopped into small pieces (optional)

100g **cucumber**, finely diced

a handful of **fresh coriander**, roughly chopped

freshly squeezed lemon juice

salt

This nutty lentil salad is very moreish. In the southern states of India it is made with raw split mung beans, soaked for a few hours, but we are a bit wary of eating raw pulses, so prefer to simmer ours for half an hour first.

Place the yellow mung dal in a pan, cover with fresh cold water and bring to a brisk boil. Reduce the heat and simmer for 30 minutes, until tender but not falling apart, skimming off any scum that rises to the surface.

Meanwhile, heat the oil in a small frying pan over a medium heat. Add the mustard seeds and, when they start to pop, add the curry leaves, coconut and nuts and cook for 2–3 minutes, stirring constantly, just until the coconut and nuts are golden brown – don't let them burn. Remove from the heat and tip the mixture straight into a serving bowl.

Drain the lentils, then cool under cold running water. Add to the bowl, along with the cucumber, coriander leaves and a little squeeze of lemon. Add a small pinch of salt, then toss and taste, adding more salt or lemon as needed. Serve immediately.

≡ TIP ≡

You can make this with or without the lentils, and grated raw beetroot or carrot is a delicious addition, as is a dollop of plain yoghurt as a dressing. Spice it up by adding finely chopped green chilli when you crackle the mustard seeds.

KACHUMBER SALAD

25g **shallots**, finely chopped

75g **cherry tomatoes**, finely chopped

50g **cucumber**, finely chopped

freshly squeezed lemon juice

salt

a handful of **fresh coriander leaves**, to garnish

A crunchy raw relish to go with your curry. Or in a sandwich. Or sprinkled over Curry Chips (see page 210). Anywhere you fancy, really.

Tip the shallots into a bowl and sprinkle over a pinch of salt. Toss and let stand for 5–10 minutes – this softens the onions and mellows their flavour. Rinse and drain.

Add the tomatoes and cucumber, squeeze over a little lemon and then taste – it shouldn't need any more salt. Finish by scattering over the coriander leaves and serve immediately.

TIP

Drizzle this with mustard oil – easily found in Asian shops – for an extra burst of peppery flavour.

CHAI MASALA

SERVES 2

PREP TIME: 5 MINS • COOK TIME: 10 MINS

WF • GF • V • DF (if substituting milk) **• NF • SoF** (unless using nut or soy milk)

4 **green cardamom pods**

8 **black peppercorns**

4 **cloves**

250ml **water**

3cm stick of **cinnamon**

¼ teaspoon **ground ginger**

1 **strongly flavoured tea bag**, torn open,
   or 1½ teaspoons **strongly flavoured
   loose-leaf tea**

250ml **whole milk** (or experiment with
   non-dairy milk)

sugar, **honey**, **maple syrup** or **agave
   nectar**, to taste

Rebecca's first taste of chai was on a train winding its way through the state of Karnataka, just outside Mumbai. It is served from tea kettles by chai wallahs who move up and down the trains, pouring out little cups of sweetly spiced tea.

If using non-dairy milk you will need to experiment – some will split when boiled, so it may be safer to gently warm it separately and then mix the chai together off the heat.

Place the cardamom pods in a pestle and mortar and bash lightly, then pop out the seeds (discarding the pods). Add the peppercorns and cloves and pummel to a coarse powder.

Place the water in a pan and set over a high heat. Add the freshly ground spices, cinnamon stick, ground ginger and tea leaves. Bring up to the boil, then remove from the heat. Stir in the milk, then bring back to the boil again.

Remove from the heat and strain into cups. Sweeten to taste.

TIP

Don't use posh or delicate tea for this. We use PG Tips at home, but any robust blend will work.

MINT & GINGER FIZZ

SERVES 8–12

PREP TIME: 5 MINS • COOK TIME: 8 MINS

WF • GF • DF • V • Ve • NF • SoF

FOR THE SYRUP:

150ml **water**

4cm piece of **ginger**, peeled and cut into matchsticks

150g **sugar**

TO SERVE:

ice

mint sprigs

soda water or **sparkling water**

salt

A refreshing and summery drink.

To make the syrup, pour the water into a saucepan and bring to a gentle boil over a medium heat. Add the ginger and simmer for 1 minute or so, then add the sugar. Stir to dissolve the sugar, then remove from the heat and set aside to cool.

Strain into a sterilized bottle or jar with a lid, to store. The syrup will keep in the fridge for about 1 week.

To serve, pour about 1 tablespoon of the syrup into a tall glass filled with ice. Take a mint sprig and place it on your palm, then clap your hands together, to release the oils. Place into the glass. Top up with fizzy water, add a tiny pinch of salt, stir and then taste – add more syrup for a sweeter, more peppery drink. Serve immediately.

LASSI

100ml **full-fat plain yoghurt** (can be non-dairy)

100ml **chilled milk** (can be non-dairy)

50ml **chilled water**

FOR MANGO LASSI:

3 tablespoons **mango purée** or mashed **fresh mango**

½ teaspoon **sugar**, or more, to taste (optional)

FOR SALTED LASSI:

a pinch of **salt**

a pinch of **dry-roasted ground cumin**

FOR SWEET LASSI:

½ teaspoon **sugar**, or more, to taste

a pinch of **saffron threads**

¼ teaspoon **rose water**, or more, to taste

≡ TIP ≡

If you have a strong enough blender, you can swap the water for 4 ice cubes, and blend until smooth and very cold.

This classic, cooling yoghurt drink can be made sweet, salty or fruity.

If using mashed fresh mango, then you will need to prepare this in a blender, but all the others can be made using a whisk.

Blend or whisk all the ingredients together, then taste – how much sweetness or other flavourings you add is very much down to personal taste, or to the ripeness of the mango.

BREAD

NAAN

MAKES 8 BREADS
PREP TIME: 20 MINS, PLUS 2 HOURS 20 MINS RISING/PROVING • COOK TIME: 6 MINS PER BREAD
V • Ve • DF (if substituting yoghurt and ghee) **• NF • SUITABLE FOR FREEZING**

2 teaspoons **dried active yeast**

215ml **lukewarm water**

2 teaspoons **sugar**

5 tablespoons **full-fat plain yoghurt** (you can use non-dairy yoghurt)

3 tablespoons **ghee** (vegan or dairy-based), melted, plus extra for brushing

400g **strong white bread flour**

100g **plain flour**, plus extra for dusting

1 teaspoon **fine salt**

neutral oil, for oiling bowl

1–2 teaspoons **nigella seeds** (optional)

═ TIP ═

To get the soft, chewy naans you'll recognize from takeaways, cool (or even freeze) the breads, then mist lightly with water and microwave for 30–40 seconds before serving.

Pillowy, slightly charred breads, served warm and brushed with ghee.

Mix the yeast, water and sugar together in a bowl and leave for 10 minutes or so for the yeast to wake up; the liquid will become frothy. Stir in the yoghurt and ghee, whisking until smooth.

In a large bowl, mix together the flours and salt. Pour in the yeast mixture and mix with a spoon until a rough dough forms. Use your hands to help bring the dough together into a soft, sticky ball. Flour a clean work surface, and knead the dough for 4–5 minutes (or use a mixer fitted with a dough hook). When it is smooth, stretchy and pliable, tip the dough into a clean oiled bowl, cover with a damp tea towel or clingfilm and leave somewhere warm to rise until doubled in size, 1–2 hours.

Turn out the dough onto the floured surface and use a sharp knife to cut in half, then divide again and again until you have 8 equal pieces. Shape into neat balls and place on a baking sheet to prove for 20 minutes or so, covered in a tea towel or loosely with clingfilm.

When ready to cook, set the oven to a low (warming) heat and set a large (ideally heavy cast-iron) frying pan over the highest heat. Let the pan get really hot while you roll out the dough.

Place a dough ball on the floured surface and flour your hands and a rolling pin. Squash the ball flat with your hands, squishing and patting it out to a circle. Pick up the dough and let gravity stretch it into an oval, turning the dough by 180° so it becomes longer. When it is about 20cm long, place it on the surface and roll out

☰ VARIATIONS ☰

FOR GARLIC NAAN: blanch 1 clove of **garlic** in boiling water for 3 minutes, then crush and mix with melted **ghee** and chopped **coriander**. Brush the mixture over the cooked naan.

FOR CHEESE NAAN: shred 1 ball of **mozzarella** and mix with **salt**, **pepper**, crushed **garlic**, chopped **shallot** or **spring onion** and **chilli flakes**. Sprinkle over a layer of cheese after rolling out the dough, then fold and gently roll it out again. Cook as here.

FOR PESHWARI NAAN: mix 5 tablespoons each of **ground almonds** and **desiccated coconut** with 2 tablespoons **sultanas** (optional), 4 tablespoons melted **ghee** or **butter**, or more if needed, and 2 teaspoons **caster sugar**, until it forms a thick paste. Squash a dough ball flat, then place a generous tablespoon of filling into the centre before folding the edges in, to form a ball again. Gently roll out and cook as here. Beware: they'll be extremely hot on the inside as they will puff up and fill with scalding steam.

to 5mm thick and about 23 x 25cm. Don't worry if this seems thin – it will puff up during cooking.

Dust off excess flour from the dough, then carefully place in the hot dry frying pan. Cook for about 2 minutes, until the bottom of the dough is freckled with brown spots and bubbles have appeared on top, then flip. Do this again once or twice, until the bubbles are just beginning to scorch, but don't allow the bread to burn.

Remove from the pan and brush lightly with melted ghee, then sprinkle over a pinch of nigella seeds, if using. Keep warm, wrapped in a tea towel in the low oven, until all the breads are cooked.

ROTI & CHAPATI

SERVES 4 (MAKES 8 BREADS)
PREP TIME: 15 MINS • COOK TIME: 3 MINS PER BREAD
DF • V • Ve • NF • SoF • SUITABLE FOR FREEZING

275g **chapati/atta flour** (or 50:50 **wholemeal** and **plain flour**), plus extra for dusting

1/3 teaspoon **fine salt**

about 150ml **water**

2 teaspoons **neutral cooking oil**

Roti and chapati are very similar flatbreads and go with almost any Indian-style curry. Since they are unleavened they take almost no time to make.

In a large bowl, stir together the flour and salt. Add enough of the water to form a dough (it shouldn't be sticky, so you may not need it all) and the oil. Bring together with your hands and, when it forms a rough ball, tip it onto a clean, floured work surface. Knead for 4–5 minutes, until the dough feels smooth and springy (or use a mixer fitted with a dough hook). Don't skimp on the time needed for this step – you need to stretch out the gluten or the finished breads will be tough.

Divide the dough into 8 equal pieces and shape into neat balls. Flour a rolling pin and the surface again and roll each ball into a 20cm disc, about 2mm thick.

Place a large frying pan over a medium-high heat. When hot, place the first bread into the dry pan. Cook for about 1 minute, or until little bubbles appear on the base of the bread. Flip, then repeat twice more, cooking for about 30 seconds each time, until no raw patches remain and a few little bubbles have charred but the bread is still soft and floppy.

Wrap the bread in a clean tea towel and keep warm while you cook the rest. Use a sheet of kitchen paper to carefully wipe away any charred flour collecting in the pan.

Serve the breads warm, to scoop up saucy curries or dhal.

TIP

To make your roti puff up, once cooked, place each one in the flame of a gas ring for 10 seconds (but be careful they don't catch and burn).

METHI THEPLA

MAKES 8 BREADS

PREP TIME: 20 MINS • COOK TIME: 5 MINS PER BREAD

DF • V • Ve (if substituting yoghurt) • **NF • SoF** (unless using nut or soy yoghurt) • **SUITABLE FOR FREEZING**

200g **chapati/atta flour** or **wholemeal plain flour**

50g **white plain flour**, plus extra for dusting

25g **chickpea flour/besan** (or substitute **white plain flour**)

½ teaspoon **ground turmeric**

½ teaspoon **ground coriander**

¼ teaspoon **asafoetida** (optional, but really good)

½ teaspoon **fine salt**

4 tablespoons **full-fat plain yoghurt** (or **non-dairy yoghurt**)

up to 100ml **water**

60g **fresh** or **frozen fenugreek leaves** (not dried) (defrosted and excess water squeezed out, if frozen), finely chopped, tough stalks discarded

½ teaspoon **peeled and finely grated ginger**

1 teaspoon **neutral cooking oil**, plus extra for frying

═ TIP ═

Many recipes for methi thepla include finely chopped green chilli, chilli flakes or chilli powder, or coriander leaves, so feel free to experiment.

These delicious flatbreads are made with chopped fenugreek leaves (methi), which we buy in frozen blocks, like spinach, in the supermarket, but you can also get them fresh in Asian food stores.

In a large bowl, stir together the flours, turmeric, coriander, asafoetida, if using, and salt. Add the yoghurt and about half the water and mix. As a rough dough starts to form, add the chopped fenugreek leaves, ginger, oil and just enough water to bring everything together – the leaves will release water as they are kneaded, so keep the dough as dry as you can.

Turn the dough onto a clean floured surface and knead for 4–5 minutes, until it feels smooth and elastic. Roll into a log shape, divide into 8 equal pieces and shape each piece into a neat ball. Using a floured rolling pin, roll each ball into a 20cm disc, about 2mm thick.

Place a large frying pan over a high heat. Use a heatproof brush or spatula to lightly coat the pan with oil, then slide in the first bread. Cook for about 2 minutes, until speckled with golden bubbles on the bottom. Brush the top of the bread with oil and flip over. Cook for another 2 minutes until golden bubbles appear on that side too. If any raw-looking spots remain, flip once or twice more.

Wrap the breads in a clean tea towel and keep warm while you cook the rest. Serve immediately.

RINKU'S SPICY WATER BOMBS (PUCHKAS)

MAKES 30
PREP TIME: 20 MINS • COOK TIME: 10 MINS
DF • V • Ve • NF • SoF

30 **ready-made pani puri puffs** (you can buy these in large supermarkets, as well as online or in Indian food stores)

FOR THE FILLING:

3 medium **waxy potatoes**, peeled and cut into very small cubes

400g **canned black chickpeas (kala chana)**

1 **red onion**, very finely chopped

1 **green chilli** (or more, to increase the heat level), finely chopped

3 teaspoons **chaat masala spice blend**

1 teaspoon **salt**

2 tablespoons **finely chopped fresh coriander**

1 tablespoon **rapeseed oil**

FOR THE TAMARIND WATER

75ml **Tamarind Chutney** (see page 217, or use shop-bought)

½ teaspoon **chilli powder**

½ teaspoon **ground cumin**

lemon juice or **tamarind paste/ concentrate**, as needed (optional)

Rinku is one of Rebecca's friends and she served these puchkas at a party thrown by Rebecca and Steve (photographer for this book) when they opened their own studio last year. 'This incredible pop-in-the-mouth snack can be found on every street corner in Kolkata. People even compete to devour the most in the shortest time. This version comes from my parents, who have used it to entertain loved ones for decades. For our street food stall, Raastawala, we renamed them Spicy Water Bombs because of the explosion of flavours.'

To make the filling, place the cubed potatoes in a saucepan and cover with water. Bring to the boil and simmer for 10 minutes, until tender. Drain immediately and set aside to cool.

Mix the remaining ingredients for the filling together in a bowl. When the potatoes are cool, add and mix together.

To make the tamarind water, mix everything together with 125ml water to form a loose sauce. Taste – it should be quite tangy. Add a squeeze of lemon juice or a teaspoon of tamarind paste or concentrate, if needed.

To assemble: just before serving (to avoid soggy puchkas), take each pani puri puff and gently knock a hole in the middle of one side with the back of a teaspoon. Repeat with all the puffs. Spoon 1 teaspoon of filling into each puff.

To eat, pour about 2 teaspoons of tamarind water into the filled puff and immediately pop into the mouth. Or simply serve with the water alongside.

PARATHA

MAKES 8 SMALL BREADS (OR 4–6 LARGER BREADS)
PREP TIME: 30 MINS, PLUS 30 MINS RESTING AND 15 MINS CHILLING • COOK TIME: 5 MINS PER BREAD
V • NF • SoF • SUITABLE FOR FREEZING

150g **chapati/atta flour**

50g **plain flour**, plus extra for dusting

½ teaspoon **salt**

6 tablespoons **ghee**, melted

100–125ml **water**

These flaky Indian flatbreads are a real treat. The way they are coiled and rolled out before cooking gives the dough rich, buttery layers.

Place the flours in a bowl, add the salt and 2 tablespoons of the ghee and use your hands to rub the fat in, until it feels sandy. Add enough water to make a dough, adding it little by little so it doesn't become sticky. Shape into a ball and knead for a full 5 minutes (or use a mixer fitted with a dough hook). Wrap in clingfilm or a clean damp tea towel, and let rest for 30 minutes.

With the remaining melted ghee nearby, divide the dough into 8 small balls (or 4–6 larger balls). Dust a work surface and rolling pin with flour and roll out each ball to a thin 23cm disc. Sprinkle with flour, then use a pastry brush to lightly brush the tops with melted ghee. Tightly roll up the discs into sausage shapes, then coil into spirals. Tuck the outside ends underneath the spirals.

Place in the fridge for 15 minutes to firm up (or in the freezer for 5 minutes).

Remove the coils from the fridge and dust everything with flour again. Squash each coil flat with the palm of your hand, then roll out to 20cm discs. Stack the discs with greaseproof paper between each one to stop them sticking.

When ready to cook, set a large dry frying pan over a medium heat. When hot, brush the top of one of the breads with melted ghee and place in the pan, ghee-side down. After about 2 minutes, when bubbles appear on the top, brush that side with ghee, and flip. Cook until beginning to brown, then flip again. Flip once or twice more, until the bread is golden brown all over. Set aside and keep warm while you cook the rest. Serve immediately.

≡ TIP ≡

Ghee is an Indian cooking fat made from butter, although there are vegan versions available in large supermarkets. It's easy to find, but if you can't, use unsalted butter or even cooking oil instead, making sure to wipe out the pan after cooking each bread, as leftover butter will burn. Chapati flour is also easy to find in large supermarkets, Asian food stores and online – if not, use a 50:50 mixture of wholemeal flour and plain flour.

RINKU'S PEA-STUFFED PARATHA

MAKES 15 FLATBREADS
PREP TIME: 30 MINS, PLUS 30 MINS RESTING TIME • COOK TIME: 10 MINS, PLUS 6 MINS PER BREAD
DF • V • Ve • NF • SoF

FOR THE DOUGH:

500g **chapati/atta flour**

500g **plain flour**, plus extra for dusting

¼ teaspoon **salt**

1 teaspoon **rapeseed oil**

FOR THE FILLING:

500g **frozen peas**, defrosted

4cm piece of **ginger**, peeled and finely grated

½ **red** or **green chilli**, finely chopped (optional)

½ teaspoon **salt**

1 tablespoon **rapeseed oil**

1 teaspoon **cumin seeds**

2 teaspoons **asafoetida**

TIP

This is a brilliant way to surreptitiously get an extra green vegetable into the tummies of small children.

These delicious flatbreads are Rinku's mother-in-law's recipe, and a family favourite. They are easy to cook and great to make with kids.

To make the dough, place the flours and salt in a bowl and mix well. Add the oil and a tablespoon of lukewarm water. Mix and add water a dash at a time, to form a soft dough and no flour remains on your hands. Tip out onto a floured surface and knead for 4–5 minutes (or use a mixer fitted with a dough hook). Cover with a damp tea towel and let rest for 30 minutes.

To make the filling, place the peas, ginger, chilli, if using, and salt in a food processor. Blitz briefly, until combined but still coarse, with plenty of chunks of pea left. Heat the oil in a frying pan over a medium heat. Add the cumin seeds and cook just until fragrant, taking care not to burn them. Add the pea mixture and stir-fry gently for 5 minutes. Stir in the asafoetida and cook until the mixture begins to look dry and a little crumbly, about 5–10 minutes. Remove from the heat and let cool.

Shape the dough into 15 equal balls. Flatten one with both palms into a disc, then press your thumb against the edges, to make thinner and larger. Hold the disc in your cupped palm and fill with 2 teaspoons of pea filling. Bring the sides of the dough into the centre and pinch the edges to seal. Repeat for all 15 portions, then gently roll each ball out on a floured surface to about 20cm in diameter, taking care not to roll so hard that the filling breaks through.

Place a frying pan over a medium heat. When hot, cook a paratha for 2–3 minutes, or until it begins to change colour and a few brown spots appear on the bottom. Flip, brush the top with ¼ teaspoon oil, cook this side and repeat. Remove from the pan, wrap in foil and keep warm while you cook the rest. Serve immediately.

RINKU'S EGG KATI ROLL

MAKES 4
PREP TIME: 15 MINS • COOK TIME: 5 MINS PER KATI ROLL
V • NF • SoF (check paratha ingredients)

½ **cucumber**, cut into thin julienne slices

1 **onion**, finely sliced

2 **red chillies**, deseeded and finely chopped

1 tablespoon **freshly squeezed lime juice** (about ½ lime)

4 **eggs**

salt

2 tablespoons **neutral cooking oil** (optional)

4 **parathas** or **other flatbreads** (homemade, see pages 205–6 or 198–201, or ready-made), uncooked

½ teaspoon **black salt** (optional)

lime wedges, to serve

Raastawaala – Rinku's street food stall – is famous for selling kati rolls. 'For every Bengali from Kolkata, this egg kati roll holds a special place. Traditionally bought by workers on their way home as a filler until their next meal, now tourists from all over the world make a point to try (and re-try) one. You can use lots of other fillings. Almost any leftover Indian-style curry will work: try chana masala, keema, sag paneer or chicken tikka masala, as well as raita.'

Place the cucumber, onion and chillies in a bowl. Squeeze over half the lime juice and mix, then set aside to allow the ingredients to pickle lightly. In another bowl, crack one of the eggs and whisk it with a pinch of salt.

Place a medium frying pan over a medium heat. When hot, and if using homemade paratha, add 1½ teaspoons of oil. (If you're using ready-made paratha, you can probably cook directly in a dry, non-stick pan.) Place a paratha into the hot pan and cook until golden spots begin to appear on the underside. Flip and cook the other side until it starts to turn golden, then use tongs to lift the bread from the pan.

Pour the beaten egg into the pan, spreading it out quickly to the size of the paratha, then place the partly cooked paratha directly on top. Press down gently, to ensure that both the bread and the egg cook fully, about 1 minute. Remove and keep warm while you cook the rest in the same way.

To assemble: place a sheet of greaseproof paper on a plate and then a paratha, egg side up. Sprinkle with a pinch of black salt, if using. Add a row of pickled salad, followed by a squeeze of lime juice. Roll up, using the greaseproof paper to enclose the roll and twisting the sheet at the end. Repeat for all the parathas and serve.

≡ TIP ≡

In Kolkata, tomato ketchup is often served with kati rolls, to use as a dip or drizzle. Parathas are quite rich, so you can substitute rotis or chapatis, if wished.

CURRY WRAPS & CURRY CHIPS

. . . .

Leftover curry is a real treat – and is often better than when freshly made.

. . . .

CURRY CHIPS

. . . .

SERVES 4

PREP TIME: 20–30 MINS • COOK TIME: 20 MINS

Can be WF • GF • DF • V • Ve • NF • SoF

. . . .

750g **oven chips** or **baked fries**,
  uncooked
8 heaped serving spoons **leftover saucy
  curry** – Chana Masala (page 94) is
  particularly good, but any will work

TO SERVE:
Raita (pages 163 or 164)
one or all of the following chutneys:
  Mango Chutney (page 216), **Lime Pickle**
  (page 214) or **Coriander Chutney**
  (page 215)
Indian-style salad – we love the pickled
  onions from Rinku's Egg Kati Rolls (page
  209) or Kachumber Salad (page 192)
fresh coriander
finely sliced **red chillies**

Who says curry has to be with rice? We've been serving baked fries at LEON since 2012 – they go with everything.

. . . .

Cook the chips or fries according to the directions on the packet.

Meanwhile, reheat the curry until piping hot.

Serve the fries topped with the curry, garnished generously with chutney(s), raita, Indian salads, coriander leaves and chillies. Devour. Ideally with beer.

CURRY WRAPS

SERVES 4
PREP TIME: 15 MINS • COOK TIME: 5–10 MINS
Can be **DF • V • Ve • NF • SoF**

leftover Indian-style curry, of your choice
one of the following spiced proteins:
  leftover Onion Bhaji (page 154);
  leftover Spiced Lamb Chops (page 101), meat stripped and roughly chopped;
  leftover Curry-Spiced Tofu (page 102);
  leftover Lamb Keema (page 145)
4 large **flatbreads/wraps**
4–6 sprigs of **tender mint**
a handful of **fresh coriander**
4 tablespoons **pomegranate seeds**
½ **red onion**, finely sliced
10cm piece of **cucumber**, sliced into long thin pieces
Raita (pages 163 or 164), for drizzling
one or two, or all, of the following chutneys (shopbought or homemade):
  Mango Chutney (page 216); **Coriander Chutney** (page 215); **Tamarind Chutney** (page 217); **Lime Pickle** (page 214)
finely chopped **red chillies**
4 **crisp lettuce leaves** (romaine or gem lettuces work well)

To make a good wrap, you need a mixture of firm, chunky (not saucy) curry or spiced protein, crunchy veg and sauce.

Thoroughly reheat whichever curry and/or protein you have chosen to use.

Warm the flatbreads/wraps, either in a low oven or directly over a gas ring for 30 seconds (do this as needed, for each wrap as you make them).

Lay a bread out flat in front of you (if you want to prevent leaks, lay a sheet of foil or baking paper underneath to wrap everything in at the end). Spoon one-quarter of the curry in a vertical line in the middle of the bread, starting about one-third from the bottom. Place any protein in a line next to it. Top with the herbs, pomegranate seeds and a few slices of onion and cucumber. Drizzle over some raita and any chutneys, then finish with a sprinkle of chillies and a lettuce leaf.

Fold up the bottom section of the wrap (which shouldn't have any fillings on it) to enclose about half the fillings. Fold in each side of the wrap, tightly enclosing the fillings like an envelope. If you used paper or foil, use it to wrap everything further. Repeat with the other breads. Eat immediately.

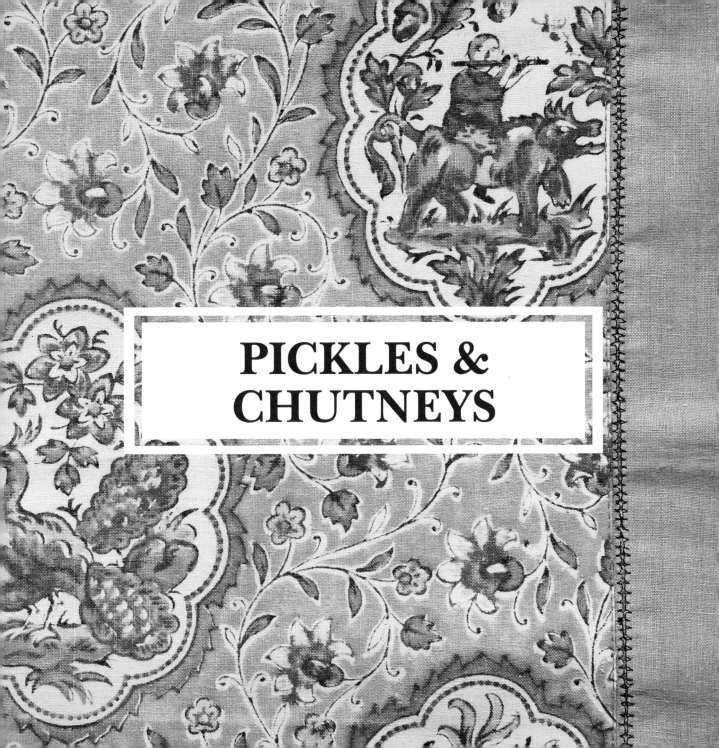

PICKLES &
CHUTNEYS

LIME PICKLE

MAKES 6–10 PORTIONS
PREP TIME: 15 MINS, PLUS UP TO 4 WEEKS PICKLING • COOK TIME: 1 MIN
WF • GF • DF • V • Ve • NF • SoF

10 **limes**, stems removed, washed throroughly

6 tablespoons **freshly squeezed lime juice** (about 3 limes)

1 teaspoon **ground turmeric**

4 cloves of **garlic**, crushed

3cm piece of **ginger**, peeled and finely grated

2½ tablespoons **fine salt**

2 tablespoons **sugar**

¼ teaspoon **asafoetida**

1½ teaspoons **hot chilli powder** (or more, to taste)

1 tablespoon **paprika**

FOR THE TEMPER:

6 tablespoons **neutral cooking oil**

1 tablespoon **black mustard seeds**

½ teaspoon **fenugreek seeds**

1 teaspoon **nigella seeds**

a pinch of **cumin seeds**

1 teaspoon **fennel seeds**

6 **curry leaves**, roughly torn

Is there anything better than a dollop of hot and sharp lime pickle next to a portion of curry or loaded onto a shard of poppadum? Yep... If it's pickle you've made yourself.

Slice each lime into 4 wedges (or 6 if large), then cut each segment into 6–8 small pieces, widthways. Place in a bowl with the remaining ingredients (except the temper) and mix well.

To make the temper, heat the oil in a small pan over a medium heat. When hot, add the mustard seeds and, when they begin to pop, add the fenugreek, nigella, cumin and fennel seeds and let sizzle for 30–50 seconds. Remove from the heat, add the curry leaves and sizzle briefly, stirring. Tip the tempered spices into the bowl with the lime. Mix well, then taste for heat levels – if you love really hot pickles, you may want to add some more chilli powder, or even crumbled dried chillies.

Pour everything into a large sterilized jar with a lid (1 litre capacity, or use 2 or 3 small jars), allowing a 3cm gap at the top. Leave for 2–4 weeks (the longer the better), turning the jar upside down every couple of days. Once opened, store in the fridge for around 1 month. Use clean spoons when serving or the chutney may go mouldy.

≡ TIP ≡

Open carefully, in the sink or wearing an apron, as the jars will release little splashes of spicy oil.

CORIANDER CHUTNEY

SERVES 4 AS A RELISH
PREP TIME: 15 MINS
WF • GF • DF • V • Ve • NF • SoF

This hot, sweet, sharp emerald-green chutney contains no artificial preservatives, so it's best to make it in small quantities and eat it quickly. We serve it alongside Indian vegetable curries, with dhal and yoghurt, in our favourite Curry Wraps (see page 211), or even slathered into a Mumbai-style sandwich. Try adding peanuts, crushed garlic, chopped chives or shallot, or even a dollop of yoghurt.

a handful of **fresh coriander leaves**, stalks removed, washed well and very finely chopped

2cm piece of **ginger**, peeled and grated

1 tablespoon **freshly squeezed lemon juice**

¼ teaspoon **ground cumin**

2 generous pinches of **asafoetida** (optional)

2 tablespoons **oil** (**vegetable**, **sunflower**, **olive** or **rapeseed**)

1 teaspoon **sugar**

½–1 small **hot green chilli**, deseeded and finely chopped, to taste

¼ teaspoon **hot chilli powder** (optional)

¼–½ teaspoon **fine salt**

Place all the ingredients except the chilli powder, and using only ¼ teaspoon salt to start with, into a pestle and mortar or into a tall container to fit a hand-held stick blender. Pound or blitz very well, until about as smooth as pesto. Taste and decide if you want to add the rest of the salt or the chilli powder, or even more sugar or lemon. It should be tangy, sharp, a little salty and a little sweet, with a good level of heat from the chilli.

Store in a lidded container in the fridge, for no more than 2 days. A layer of oil or clingfilm pressed over the top will help prevent the coriander discolouring.

MANGO CHUTNEY

MAKES 2 X 400G JARS
PREP TIME: 20 MINS • COOK TIME: 1 HOUR
WF • GF • DF • V • Ve • NF • SoF

a pinch of **cumin seeds**

a pinch of **coriander seeds**

4 **green cardamom pods**

200ml **white wine vinegar** or **apple cider vinegar**

225g **sugar**

1½ teaspoons **fine salt**

4cm piece of **ginger**, peeled and finely grated

1 clove of **garlic**, crushed

a pinch of **nigella seeds**

½ teaspoon **paprika**

2 ripe **mangos**

Fruuuuuuuity. And not too sweet.

In a hot dry pan, toast the cumin seeds, coriander seeds and cardamom pods for 1 minute or so, until just fragrant. Tip into a pestle and mortar and bruise lightly. Set aside.

Place the vinegar, sugar, salt, ginger and garlic in a deep non-reactive pan and bring to a simmer, stirring until the sugar dissolves. Add the bruised spices, along with the nigella seeds and paprika. Reduce the heat and simmer while you prepare the mangos.

If the mangos are very ripe, work over a large bowl to catch all the lovely juices. Using a small sharp knife, cut a line around the middle of the mango, then do the same lengthways. Peel off one-quarter of the skin and cut chunks of the flesh away from the stone. Repeat with the next quarter and, when the stone is revealed, trim away as much flesh as you can. Repeat until all 4 quarters have been cut away from the stone. Cut the flesh into 1–2cm pieces.

Add the fruit and any collected juices to the pan and bring back to the boil. Cook for 50–60 minutes over a medium heat, carefully stirring often so the bottom doesn't burn, until reduced by about half and nicely thickened.

While piping hot, carefully pour into clean sterilized jars and immediately cover with lids. It will keep for months, sealed. After opening, store in the fridge and use within 2–3 weeks.

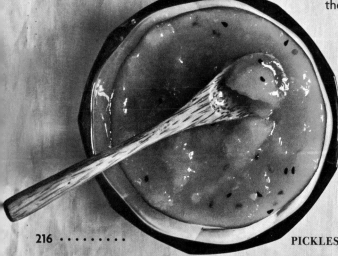

COCONUT CHUTNEY

SERVES 4 AS A RELISH
PREP TIME: 8 MINS • COOK TIME: 3 MINS
WF • GF • DF • V • Ve • NF • SoF

Delicious with everything from samosas to bhajis.

1 tablespoon **vegetable oil**

2 teaspoons **mustard seeds**

a generous pinch of **cumin seeds**

1 teaspoon grated **ginger**

8 tablespoons **desiccated coconut**

100ml **freshly boiled water**, or more as needed

a pinch of **salt**

Heat the oil in a small pan over a medium heat. When hot, add the mustard and cumin seeds and toast, just until they begin to crackle. Remove from the heat, stir the ginger into the pan and let sizzle.

Tip the desiccated coconut into a bowl and add the freshly boiled water, along with the toasted spices and salt. Mix together and add more boiling water until you get a good consistency – it should be thick rather than watery, but not stiff. Leave to cool before serving.

RINKU'S EASY TAMARIND CHUTNEY

MAKES ABOUT 100ML
PREP TIME: 5 MINS • COOK TIME: 7 MINS
WF • GF • DF • V • VE • NF • SoF

'This chutney is a sweet, sour, tangy brown sauce. It's super popular in India and goes with almost anything (I think of it as a ketchup equivalent). Drizzle it on savoury dishes, or serve as a dip. Traditionally, it is made with dried tamarind, which is boiled and reduced for hours – this is my easy version.'

1½ teaspoons **cumin seeds**

5 tablespoons **tamarind paste** (choose a good-quality paste with no fibrous strands)

3 tablespoons **jaggery** or any **dark sugar**

1 teaspoon **chilli powder**

½ teaspoon **salt**

4 tablespoons **water**

Dry-roast the cumin seeds in a frying pan over a medium heat, just until fragrant. Grind to a powder in a pestle and mortar.

Place the ground cumin and all the other ingredients into a saucepan, mix well and bring to the boil. Reduce the heat and simmer for about 5 minutes, until the chutney thickens. Remove from the heat and let cool.

When cool, place into a clean sterilized jar and seal. The chutney can be refrigerated for up to 2 weeks.

INDEX

A

aloo tikki 158

Asian greens: steamed greens 180

Thai-style fried rice 175

see also pak choi

asparagus: chicken meatball coconut
curry 71

aubergines: aubergine and tomato
curry 125

jungle curry 49

lemongrass coconut aubergine

curry 80

B

balti: Emily's amazing Birmingham balti
149–51

beans *see* black beans; green beans;
kidney beans

beef: beef Madras 53

beef rendang 131

Cape Malay curried beef 34

massaman curry 22

Shumaiya's akhni pilau 177

beetroot: beetroot and coconut
curry 63

beetroot thoran 184

Rinku's beetroot pachadi 167

Bengali fish tenga 29

bhajis: onion bhajis 154

bhuna: fish bhuna 113

Birmingham balti 149–51

biryani: chicken biryani 146–8

black beans: Caribbean-style black bean
curry 57

coconut rice 'n' peas 178

black dhal makhani 135

Bombay potatoes 187

bread: curry wraps 211

methi thepla 201

naan 198–9

paratha 205

Rinku's egg kati roll 209

Rinku's pea-stuffed paratha 206

Rinku's spicy water bombs 202

roti and chapati 200

broccoli: steamed greens 180

tofu phad phrik khing 97

Burmese-style fish, prawn and tomato
curry 109

butternut squash: butternut, chickpea
and kale curry 136

Erica's lentil masala 72

C

'ca ri ga' Vietnamese chicken curry 21

cabbage, pea and potato curry 183

cafreal: Chiara's grandmother's Goan
chicken cafreal 54

Cape Malay curried beef 34

Caribbean chicken and mango curry
30

Caribbean-style black bean curry 57

cauliflower: baked aloo gobi 188

cauliflower rice 170

quickest curry ever 98

Sri Lankan-style jackfruit curry 121

chai masala 193

chana masala 94

chapati 200

cheese: cheese naan 199

sag paneer 60

chicken: 1960s chicken tikka masala 16–17

'ca ri ga' Vietnamese chicken curry 21

Caribbean chicken and mango
curry 30

Chiara's grandmother's Goan chicken
cafreal 54

chicken biryani 146–8

chicken chettinad 76

chicken dopiaza 142

chicken meatball coconut curry 71

Colombo de Martinique 33

doro alicha'a tibs 117

Emily's amazing Birmingham baltim
149–51

jungle curry 49

kuku paka with ugali 138–9

Nilgiri curry 67

Shumaiya's family chicken korma 64

Thérèse's chicken katsu and curry
sauce 25

chickpeas: butternut, chickpea and kale
curry 136

chana masala 94

Rinku's spicy water bombs 202

West African-style peanut curry 84

chillies 10

chips: curry chips 210

chutneys: coconut chutney 217

coriander chutney 215

mango chutney 216

Rinku's easy tamarind chutney 217

clams: Thai-style clam curry 122

coconut: beetroot and coconut
curry 63

chicken meatball coconut curry 71
coconut chutney 217
coconut rice 168
coconut rice 'n' peas 178
coconut sticky cauliflower rice 170
lemongrass coconut aubergine
  curry 80
Sri Lankan-style coconut dhal 79
Colombo de Martinique 33
coriander: coriander chutney 215
  Nilgiri curry 67
  Rinku's pomegranate and coriander
    raita 164
corn: chicken meatball coconut
  curry 71
  jungle curry 49
cornershop curry 90
cornmeal: kuku paka with ugali 138–9
courgettes: skinny parcel-baked salmon
  and courgette curry 89
  South Indian-style fish curry 83
  Sri Lankan-style green bean and
    courgette curry 106
cucumber: kachumber salad 192
cumin: jeera rice 169
curd rice 168

D dhal: black dhal makhani 135
  everyday dhal 26
  Sri Lankan-style coconut dhal 79
dhansak: lamb dhansak 132
dopiaza: chicken dopiaza 142
doro alicha'a tibs 117
drinks: chai masala 193

lassi 195
mint and ginger fizz 194

E eggs: curry udon noodles 14
  egg-fried rice with soy sauce 173
  gym bunny curry 114
  Rinku's egg kati roll 209
everyday dhal 26

F fenugreek leaves: Matt's lamb keema 145
  methi thepla 201
fish and seafood: baked mackerel
  curry 93
  Burmese-style fish, prawn and tomato
    curry 109
  cornershop curry 90
  curried prawn stir-fry 118
  fish bhuna 113
  Lipu's Bengali fish tenga 29
  skinny parcel-baked salmon and
    courgette curry 89
  South Indian-style fish curry 83
  Thai fishcakes 157
  Thai-style clam curry 122

G gap year curry 44–6
garlic naan 199
ginger: mint and ginger fizz 194
Goan chicken cafreal 54
goat: heartbreak curry 38–9
green beans: chicken meatball coconut
  curry 71
  cornershop curry 90
  jungle curry 49

quickest curry ever 98
Sri Lankan-style green bean and
  courgette curry 106
Sri Lankan-style jackfruit curry 121
steamed greens 180
tofu phad phrik khing 97
green curry 44–6
greens 11
  baked mackerel curry 93
  kuku paka with ugali 138–9
  steamed greens 180
  tofu phad phrik khing 97
  see also Asian greens; broccoli; chard;
    kale; spinach
gungo peas: coconut rice 'n' peas 178
gym bunny curry 114

H heartbreak curry 38–9

I Indian-style cauliflower rice 170
Indian-style fried rice 174
Indian-style steamed greens 180

J jackfruit 11
  Sri Lankan-style jackfruit curry 121
jalfrezi: vegetable jalfrezi 98
Japanese-style cauliflower rice 170
jeera rice 169
jungle curry 49

K kachumber salad 192
kale: butternut, chickpea and kale
  curry 136
  West African-style peanut curry 84

katsu: Thérèse's chicken katsu and curry sauce 25
keema: Matt's lamb keema 145
khao soi gai 75
kidney beans: black dhal makhani 135
coconut rice 'n' peas 178
rajma 110
korma: Shumaiya's family chicken korma 64
koshambari salad 191
kuku paka with ugali 138–9

L
lamb: heartbreak curry 38–9
lamb dhansak 132
lamb pasanda 68
lamb rogan josh 128
Matt's lamb keema 145
Shumaiya's akhni pilau 177
smoky curry-spiced lamb chops 101
lassi 195
lemongrass coconut aubergine curry 80
lentils: black dhal makhani 135
Erica's lentil masala 72
everyday dhal 26
koshambari salad 191
lamb dhansak 132
Sri Lankan-style coconut dhal 79
lime pickle 214

M
mackerel: baked mackerel curry 93
cornershop curry 90
Madras curry: beef Madras 53
mangetout: steamed greens 180
mangos: Caribbean chicken and

mango curry 30
mango chutney 216
mango lassi 195
massaman curry 22
meatballs: chicken meatball coconut curry 71
methi: Matt's lamb keema 145
methi thepla 201
mint: mint and ginger fizz 194
Nilgiri curry 67
mozzarella: cheese naan 199
mung/moong dal: koshambari salad 191
mushrooms: curry udon noodles 14
mutton: heartbreak curry 38–9

N
naan 198–9
Nilgiri curry 67
noodles: crunchy deep-fried noodles 74
curry udon noodles 14
khao soi gai 75

O
onions: chicken dopiaza 142
crispy onions 179
onion bhajis 154
see also shallots

P
pachadi: Rinku's beetroot pachadi 167
pak choi: chicken meatball coconut curry 71
steamed greens 180
pakora see bhajis
paneer 11
sag paneer 60
paratha 205

Rinku's egg kati roll 209
Rinku's pea-stuffed paratha 206
parcel-baked salmon and courgette curry 89
pasanda: lamb pasanda 68
peanut butter: West African-style peanut curry 84
peas: cabbage, pea and potato curry 183
Matt's lamb keema 145
pea and potato samosas 161–2
Rinku's pea-stuffed paratha 206
steamed greens 180
peppers: quickest curry ever 98
peshwari naan 199
pickles: lime pickle 214
pilau: Shumaiya's akhni pilau 177
polenta: kuku paka with ugali 138–9
pomegranate and coriander raita 164
pork: pork vindaloo 50
Thai red curry with crispy pork belly 43
potatoes: aloo tikki 158
baked aloo gobi 188
baked mackerel curry 93
Bombay potatoes 187
cabbage, pea and potato curry 183
curry chips 210
massaman curry 22
pea and potato samosas 161–2
Rinku's spicy water bombs 202
prawns: Burmese-style fish, prawn and tomato curry 109
curried prawn stir-fry 118
puchkas 202

purple-sprouting broccoli: steamed greens 180

Q
quickest curry ever 98

R
raita 163
 Rinku's pomegranate and coriander raita 164
rajma 110
red curry with crispy pork belly 43
rendang: beef rendang 131
rice: basic steamed white rice 9
 black rice 169
 cauliflower rice 170
 chicken biryani 146–8
 coconut rice 168
 coconut rice 'n' peas 178
 curd rice 168
 egg-fried rice with soy sauce 173
 Indian-style fried rice 174
 jeera rice 169
 Shumaiya's akhni pilau 177
 Thai-style fried rice 175
rogan josh: lamb rogan josh 128
roti 200

S
sag paneer 60
salmon: Burmese-style fish, prawn and tomato curry 109
 skinny parcel-baked salmon and courgette curry 89
salted lassi 195
samosas: pea and potato samosas 161–2
seafood see fish and seafood

seitan 11
shallots: kachumber salad 192
South Indian-style fish curry 83
soy sauce: egg-fried rice with soy sauce 173
spices 10
 see also individual spices
spinach: baked mackerel curry 93
 sag paneer 60
split peas see yellow split peas
Sri Lankan-style coconut dhal 79
Sri Lankan-style green bean and courgette curry 106
Sri Lankan-style jackfruit curry 121
sugar-snap peas: steamed greens 180
sweet potatoes: West African-style peanut curry 84

T
tamarind: Rinku's easy tamarind chutney 217
 Rinku's spicy water bombs 202
 tamarind yoghurt 165
tea: chai masala 193
tenderstem broccoli: steamed greens 180
tenga: Lipu's Bengali fish tenga 29
Thai fishcakes 157
Thai food 47
Thai red curry with crispy pork belly 43
Thai-spiced tofu 105
Thai-style cauliflower rice 170
Thai-style clam curry 122
Thai-style fried rice 175
Thai-style steamed greens 180

thoran: beetroot thoran 184
tikka masala: 1960s chicken tikka masala 16–17
tofu 11
 curry udon noodles 14
 curry-spiced tofu 102
 Thai-spiced tofu 105
 tofu phad phrik khing 97
tomatoes: aubergine and tomato curry 125
 baked mackerel curry 93
 Burmese-style fish, prawn and tomato curry 109
 kachumber salad 192

U
udon noodles: curry udon noodles 14
ugali: kuku paka with ugali 138–9

V
vegetables 11
 vegetable jalfrezi 98
 see also individual vegetables
Vietnamese chicken curry 21
Vietnamese-style steamed greens 180
vindaloo: pork vindaloo 50

W
West African-style peanut curry 84
wraps: curry wraps 211

Y
yellow split peas: everyday dhal 26
 lamb dhansak 132
yoghurt: curd rice 168
 lassi 195
 raita 163
 Rinku's beetroot pachadi 167

ABOUT THE AUTHORS

REBECCA SEAL has written about food and drink for the *Financial Times*, the *Evening Standard*, the *Observer*, the *Guardian*, *Red* and *The Sunday Times*. Her cookbooks include *Istanbul: Recipes from the Heart of Turkey* and *Lisbon: Recipes from the heart of Portugal*, as well as co-authoring *LEON Happy Soups*, *LEON Happy One-pot Cooking* and *LEON Fast Vegan* with John Vincent. She is one of the food and drink experts on Channel 4's *Sunday Brunch*. She lives in London with her husband and two small daughters.

JOHN VINCENT is Co-founder of LEON, which now has more than 60 restaurants (including in Amsterdam, Utrecht, Oslo and Washington, DC). He wrote *LEON Naturally Fast Food* with Henry Dimbleby, *LEON Family & Friends* with Kay Plunkett-Hogge, *LEON Happy Salads* and *LEON Fast & Free* with Jane Baxter and *LEON Happy Soups*, *LEON Happy One-pot Cooking* and *LEON Fast Vegan* with Rebecca Seal. He thinks that our relationship with food should be positive and joyous and that we need to listen more carefully to our gut, eat more good fats and less sugar.

ACKNOWLEDGMENTS

JOHN

Rebecca is the most wonderful partner in the kitchen. As is Katie my partner in all the other rooms. Thank you both.

REBECCA

What a joy this book was to create. If you like food and someone suggests that you might like to work on a compilation of the best curries from around the world, you jump at the chance – I think that was true for everyone who worked on this project. First, thank you to John Vincent, for once again giving me the chance to be part of the lovely LEON family and to write this with him. Thanks also to Rebecca Di Mambro, Ottie Ise and Charlotte Baly, along with everyone at LEON who helped put this together.

The book's fabulous good looks are down to photographer Steven Joyce, food stylist Sian Henley and props stylist Lauren Law, and we couldn't have done it without the assistance of Tom Groves and Charlie Crosley-Thorne, who always go beyond the call of duty to make our shoots work perfectly. Thank you to the brilliant design team at Octopus Books for pulling it all together, as well as our Publisher Alison Starling, Creative Director Jonathan Christie and Editors Pauline Bache and Sophie Elletson, who make it all make sense.

We love being able to include recipes from our friends, and friends of LEON, and we are so grateful to Davide Ghetaceu from Ethiopian Flavours, Shumi Khan, Emily Hawkley, Thérèse Gaughan, Chiara Pinto and Erica Molyneaux for letting us include their wonderful dishes. I owe particular thanks to my friend Rinku Dutt, who gave us more recipes than anyone else and taught me a lot about curries along the way, too.

I also owe a debt of gratitude to the food writers who have inspired me over the years, and knowingly or unknowingly, their past recipes have helped us write this book: Diana Henry, Maunika Gowardan, Meera Sodha and Madhur Jaffrey in particular. I feel seriously lucky that this is my job.

An Hachette UK Company
www.hachette.co.uk

First published in Great Britain in 2019 by Conran Octopus,
an imprint of Octopus Publishing Group Ltd
Carmelite House
50 Victoria Embankment
London EC4Y 0DZ
www.octopusbooks.co.uk

ISBN 978-1-84091-791-8

A CIP catalogue record for this book is available from the British Library.

Printed and bound in China

10 9 8 7 6 5 4 3 2 1

Photography by Steven Joyce

Publisher: Alison Starling
Creative director: Jonathan Christie
Senior editors: Pauline Bache and Sophie Elletson
Copyeditor: Emily Preece-Morrison
Food styling: Sian Henley
Prop styling: Lauren Law
Designer: Ella Mclean
Senior production manager: Allison Gonsalves

We have endeavoured to be as accurate as possible in all the preparation
and cooking times listed in the recipes in this book. However, they are an
estimate based on our own timings during recipe testing, and should be
taken as a guide only, not as the literal truth.

Nutrition advice is not absolute. If you feel you require consultation
with a nutritionist, consult your GP for a recommendation.

Standard level spoon measurements are used in all recipes.
1 tablespoon = one 15ml spoon
1 teaspoon = one 5ml spoon

Eggs should be medium unless otherwise stated and preferably free
range and organic. The Department of Health advises that eggs should
not be consumed raw. This book contains dishes made with raw or lightly
cooked eggs. It is prudent for more vulnerable people such as pregnant
and nursing mothers, invalids, the elderly, babies and young children to
avoid uncooked or lightly cooked dishes made with eggs. Once prepared
these dishes should be kept refrigerated and used promptly.

Fresh herbs should be used unless otherwise stated. If unavailable, use
dried herbs as an alternative but halve the quantities stated.

Ovens should be preheated to the specific temperature – if using a
fan-assisted oven, follow manufacturer's instructions for adjusting the
time and the temperature.

This book includes dishes made with nuts and nut derivatives. It is
advisable for customers with known allergic reactions to nuts and nut
derivatives and those who may be potentially vulnerable to these aller-
gies, such as pregnant and nursing mothers, invalids, the elderly, babies
and children, to avoid dishes made with nuts and nut oils. It is also
prudent to check the labels of pre-prepared ingredients for the possible
inclusion of nut derivatives.

Vegetarians should look for the 'V' symbol on a cheese to ensure it is
made with vegetarian rennet.
Not all soy sauce is gluten-free – we use tamari (a gluten-free type of soy
sauce), but check the label if you are unsure.

Remember to check the labels on ingredients to make sure they don't
have hidden refined sugars. Even savoury goods can be artificially
sweetened so it's always best to check the label carefully.